The 8 Pillars of Social Media Marketing in 2019

By: Matthew Bartnick

Contents

Introduction

It used to be that small businesses could not compete against large businesses in the same market in an effective way because they could not afford to advertise their products or properly brand themselves because of the expense involved. Those days are long gone. These were the days of TV advertising and Print Advertising in newspapers and magazines, and even radio commercials.

Advertising has completely changed. You don't see big companies scampering to get their ads on TV, or hunt for billboards in the city. They now aim at reaching their customers the contemporary way. As you know, nowadays people get most of their news online, and conversations on the hottest topics take place in small online groups, forums, and website comment sections. Successful companies do not even need to jostle for space on radio or TV, and social media has emerged as the most powerful marketing tool out there. But then, you probably already know this, and the burning question is not what benefits social media brings, but how to use social media to harness all the benefits it offers to small businesses and large companies alike.

As a rule of thumb, you should not just dive into social media with the intent of marketing your products or building a brand; you need proper planning and a roadmap to achieve your end results. It's like going to an unknown city without a map and trying to explore all of it in one day. Does that sound feasible to you? You must first figure out how to execute your plan so that success will be guaranteed. Many marketers today make mistakes that they never really recover from; you should not join this statistic.

What do we mean by the phrase 'social media'? While the meaning may seem obvious, you probably have no specific definition of what it means. The Yale School of Music has defined social media as websites and applications that enable Internet users to create, access, and share a wide range of content, and to actively take part in social networking. Simply put, social media is a platform that allows users to communicate. This communication can take many forms, including adding comments, creating text, uploading videos and images, and interacting with what others have to share.

Social media includes social bookmarking, wikis, video and photo sharing, and social news, to mention just a few. The journey to establishing such a powerful and potent interactive platform has been long and intensive, but it is now ripe for you to take advantage of and reach the masses that are undeniably addicted and are ever more voraciously devouring content. You will see its true potential very soon! If you are still unsure why you need to embrace social media as a marketing and branding platform, perhaps you need further illustration of just why it is the best place to find and engage your target audience and to ride the wave of engagement to make your business grow.

This book will be the comprehensive social media marketing guide you've always needed in order to master, manipulate, and dominate social media, including Facebook, Twitter, Instagram, YouTube, and LinkedIn. The chapters here are structured to make it easy for you to understand the why and the how of social media marketing, and to take you from a novice entrepreneur with little to no knowledge of social media to a marketing and branding guru capable of formulating and executing winning marketing strategies for profitable entrepreneurship.

Common Features of Social Media

What connects the different social media platforms? As a rule of thumb, they all contain several varying features that are differently presented from app to app; yet still familiar to most users. The three essential features are listed below.

Profile Page: It's the essential part of a social media platform, as this is the user's way to create content and interact with others. It will usually feature a photo as well as a small description. The depth of these descriptions and profiles varies. Facebook has a relatively extended profile, featuring information about your education and family members and the like, while Instagram only allows you a 140-character description below your name. Of course this depends on what type of page you're talking about. If it's a business page, a group, or a "place," the information presented may vary. The profile page, or home page to your profile (whether personal or otherwise) is incredibly important because this is where the visitor decides to either click around to find out more information, or else abandon your profile and move on to the next thing. If you don't capture their attention and win their interest here, you'll be unlikely to convert them elsewhere.

News Feed: To see what your friends and your followed pages are posting, you'll have to check the newsfeed. Updated in real-time, your newsfeed features posts from peers and companies, which you can usually 'like', comment on or even share. While different outlets have different names for the posts, (example: Twitter referencing a share as a "retweet"), the fundamental idea is the same.

Hashtag: While you can easily see your friends' content on your feeds, the hashtag allows users to connect their content globally little more than as a symbol "#". For example, if a user has a status update on a great meal at a specific restaurant, the user can create the status update and hashtag it with the brand name, i.e. #DominosPizza or #McDonalds, thereby allowing other users to search the brand name and see the post. Hashtags have been one of the most effective ways to launch campaigns and connects users to a topic of discussion.

Who Uses Social Media?

It used to be a rule of thumb that only the younger generation was involved in social media. Yet a lot has changed from the early days of Mark Zuckerberg's brainchild Facebook, which was once upon a time restricted to only University students. Adults and children are adding to the profiles of social media users, diversifying the crowd, and changing the playing field for marketing.

With 3.4 billion Internet users around the world, 2.3billion of which are active on social media, there doesn't exist just one type of social media users. The profile and platform preference for individual social media users varies across the globe and depends on demographic factors such as age, income, education and area. The average social media user has five accounts and spends around 1 hour and 40 minutes browsing these apps daily, accounting for 28% of their time spent on the Internet.

So the short answer: EVERYONE uses social media. But as you will see throughout this book, that doesn't mean everyone uses social media the same way. Therefore, your approach will need to be tailored to the way in which your target market particularly uses the platform.

The Age Game

According to the highly acclaimed Pew Research Center, 74% of all adults online use social media since January 2014. The number is no doubt continuing its growing trend.

Social Media Use by Age Group Over Time

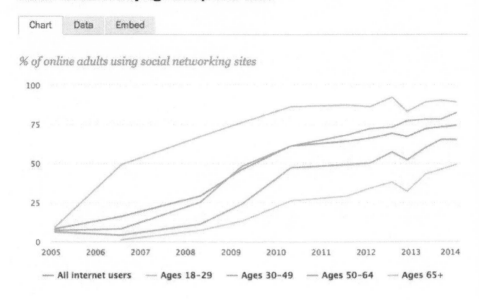

PEW RESEARCH CENTER

That number is even higher for younger adults, with a reported 89% of social media users between the ages of 18-29. While the older generation is catching on slowly but surely, the younger Generation Z, born after the turn of the millennium, is already showing different behaviors for social media usage. The current high schoolers and middle schoolers are turning a cold shoulder to Facebook, once a staple for youth. Instead, they are increasingly favoring Instagram and Snapchat. It may simply be that Facebook is older news and so many older people are now using the platform that it detracts from the once "cool" factor that drove the site to its fame.

The Gender Game

Women may be from Venus and men may hail from Mars, and it shows in their social media usage. While the differences are slight, they are important enough to create the foundations of a specific marketing plan. According to a Nielsen study, women are slightly more involved in social media than men, with 76% of female users compared to 72% male users. Women also spend more time than men on social media, averaging around 10 minutes social networking on their mobile devices compared to a little less than 7 minutes for men.

Women dominate most social media platforms by a slight margin. But they greatly outnumber males on the highly visual digital pin board known as Pinterest. Women also tend to post more on social media, going so far as having more than twice as many posts on their Facebook walls as men. They are also seemingly more popular with an average of 8% more 'friends' than men.

Female Users and Male Users of Social Media Sites pages

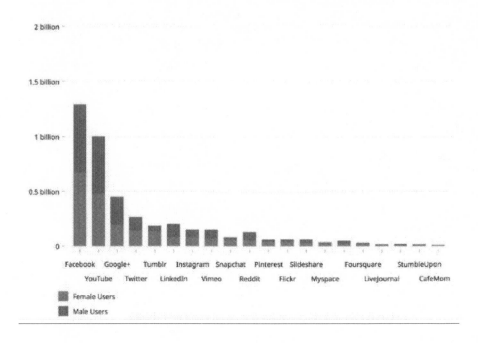

Men, however, take the lead on the professional networking site LinkedIn, which boasts 24% of the male population compared to 19% of the female population. Men are also more involved on Reddit, and more interactive on music-based social networking sites such as YouTube compared to women.

The most interesting statistic for brands that Nielsen was able to gather was that women are more engaged with brands than men and by a significant landslide. More than 50% of women use social media to show support or to access deals from brands, which is staggeringly high compared to just 36% of men who do the same. Not only do women rely more on social media to stay up to date with brands; but the ladies are also interacting more with their favored brands by comments and shares.

Why Social Media Marketing Is Important

You may perhaps have the best product in your industry. It could be the greatest thing ever made and would make a difference in someone's life. However, that does not mean people will see your creation. Your product or service may not have many sales. Without proper marketing, no one may notice what you offer. To let people see your products or services you need to promote your work with an extensive marketing campaign.

Marketing is one of the toughest things to do when it comes to running a business. Promoting your business will be more than just telling people about what you offer. You need to let people know that you exist in the first place. It is all about letting people know that what you offer is valuable and that you are available for business.

You want people to learn what your product or service is and what makes it special. Also, tell people what makes your offering worthwhile. More importantly, you need to stand out from the rest of the market. The audience needs to know why your goods or services are different from everything else on the market.

You have to get online to market your business. There's no other option. Traditional marketing avenues are starting to dry up as newspapers, and other print forms of media are not cutting it anymore. It is a matter of time before the online world becomes the only place where people search for items of their interest.

Promoting your business online is not always easy. You need to get out there and show people that you have something useful. It is all about letting the public know what you do and what you offer them.

It is often a challenge to become visible online. You might have the best business idea in the world, but that will not suffice if you are unable to market your products appropriately.

The problem with today's economy is that there always seems to be so much competition. On paper, there may be quite a few other businesses out there that provide the same product or service you provide. They might be getting more visitors to their sites than you. Others got a head start on their marketing efforts and are doing much more to market themselves than you are.

Whether you plan to run an online retail shop or a physical store, you need to know how to create an online presence. The same is true of digital products and services. It is absolutely essential to master your social media approach.

Social media has never been more popular than it is now. With social media, people can interact with each other online. They can talk about anything in some of the world's most unique digital environments. Even more importantly, people are talking with each other about the products and services they deliver. Social media became a popular promotional tool that is quickly becoming more valuable and important than any other form of traditional advertising (of course there are exceptions for certain types of products or services, but 90% of the time, this is true.)

Your social media approach can help you highlight your business in a distinctive manner.

There are many good reasons why social media marketing has become very important. Let's look at a few of these points.

Easy to Reach

Social media has dominated the online world over the years. Today, people and businesses are entering an extensive variety of sites to highlight what they offer.

People access social media sites not only with computers but also with mobile apps on their tablets and Smartphones. Even smart television sets that connect online and video game consoles with similar links can get people online too. The number of social media services that are available on these devices has been expanding in volume as well.

In addition, you can easily access other peoples' devices thanks to those social media platforms running with their own special apps. Whether it entails a traditional computer or something smaller, people are discovering new ways to use social media wherever they go. This makes it easier for people to stay in touch and to find things while on the go. With your marketing efforts, you can ensure you will be on a variety of sites to make it simpler to be spotted. And nowadays, you can reach people anywhere they are in the world on their phones.

A Diverse Layout

Social media marketing offers a diverse variety of places that target certain groups of people. No two social media platforms are alike. The differentiating and distinguishing features of each different social media platform are worth exploring. For instance, Instagram has become very popular with younger generations. They get on social media sites to share photos and short videos. LinkedIn has become attractive to professionals including people who might be trying to market extensive business programs or work-related endeavors.

Twitter helps to share messages in as few characters as possible while Pinterest examines local businesses through unique virtual storefronts.

If you do your homework, you'll find a lot of surprising insights and trends that will help you master your social media marketing approach. Start by monitoring the habits of people in your own life: colleagues, children, friends etc. Don't just go by what your own social media habits are. There are also many online tools to measure and deliver insights from social media activity.

The specific social media sites relevant to your brand will vary based on your needs, what you offer, and who you want to contact. Pinterest is ideal for arts and crafts items but not as appropriate for financial planning services, for example.

You should incorporate different strategies for each of these social media sites. These tactics vary based on how well they reach people and how you can communicate. This guide includes specifics on marketing through each of these sites. We will discuss how to do this in greater detail later in the book.

A Preferred Way to Search

One great thing about social media is that it became a popular place to find information. Just go to a social media site, and you will probably see a search engine. This feature will help you locate different businesses relating to certain keywords throughout the site.

When you use the search engine on Facebook, you will find information on Facebook profiles relating to what you specified. Facebook does this to connect you to whatever you search for. You don't even leave the site; whatever you want is already there.

In other words, people are foregoing Google and other

search engines in favor of search functions on social media sites. They know that it is easier to get in touch with people on social media. This leads to the next concept.

Localization has become a huge part of social media. When people search for things, the social media site will often give users local results first. That is, the most important results are not far from one's geographic location. This is the same as what you get from a regular search engine. Advertisers on social media can even plan their campaigns to target specific people in certain geographic areas.

Interactivity is Key

Interactivity is an important aspect when it comes to today's online world. People want to talk with others online. This includes businesses that might be promoting all sorts of things. When you access a social media site, you will do more than just tell people about your services. You will have an opportunity to talk with others. You can ask people questions or respond to their queries.

People love having others interact with them on social media. Think about all those fast food places that have their own Twitter accounts. These places often respond to people who tweet about foods they like, or to advertise their promotions. Those fast food spots love interacting because they know such interactions make them more attractive and appreciative. Whether it entails Burger King talking about some new breakfast item or Arby's inventing something new, such businesses talk about what is happening, what makes them special, and even answer questions.

Being direct with your customers is always important. When you run your business, you have to understand what consumers wish for. You must also reach out to them whenever they have questions, complaints, or compliments. Social media marketing provides an opportunity to discover what people ask for, and what interests them the most.

The old adage "the customer is always right," is worth considering here. Although it can be frustrating seeing someone post a negative review or complaint about your business publicly, this is your chance to show your professionalism. So many small businesses make the mistake of getting into arguments on social media with complainants or else they make excuses for the bad service or try to blame it on the customer. You're far better off to comment on their negative post or complaint and thank them for their constructive feedback, assure them of your apologies and that you will do everything possible to keep this from happening again, and then invite them to come back or use your service again promising them a much better experience. Even if you don't win back that customer, other people will see your grace under pressure and be much impressed. It may just win you new customers.

Always Evolving

Social media is always growing, and new outlets are introduced on a regular basis. These include places that cater to specific groups of people. For instance, the Major League Baseball sports organization formed its Infield Chatter social media system to allow baseball fans to talk about the sport, their favorite teams, and players. People can discuss the hottest stars, rising prospects, the history of the sport and so forth.

This is just one example of how social media is changing. In the future, there will be social media sites that are devoted to just about everything. There might be social media sites dedicated to people interested in arts and crafts or maybe ones that focus on certain video game consoles. Whatever the case may be, the social media field is always going to grow and change with the times.

It is impressive how the social media world works today. You will see throughout this guide that it is very easy to demonstrate your products and services to others. It's not so easy to do it in the most effective way to the right audience. In particular, you will find many options for social media sites through free and paid marketing tools that will allow you to transform your social media marketing approach with much less effort. You might be surprised how easy it is to pull off a successful campaign on social media once you've armed yourself with the knowledge and tools to do it the right way.

st Pillar: Creating your goals

...and asking, What will I get from my digital marketing efforts?

A quality social media marketing campaign will make a world of difference for your business. To make social media marketing worthwhile, examine what you are doing to get a campaign to work well and stand out. Here are some of the best ways to create a great campaign.

The first step is considering your goals for a campaign. What are you looking to get out of this campaign and how will it benefit your business? Too many people just launch into marketing campaigns or sign off on expensive advertising budgets without a clear goal in mind as to what their time and money will be used for. Are you looking to improve your relationship with customers? Do you want to increase brand recognition? Do you want to generate more traffic to your website, store or blog? Do you want to convert more of that traffic into customers? Do you want to increase the pool of repeat customers by boosting brand loyalty?

These are all questions you must consider before embarking on a campaign. Each of these goals requires a different approach. Now we'll discuss each of these goals in depth as well as strategies for attaining these goals.

Connecting Personally with your Audience: Showing Your Human Side

One of the greatest problems with trying to market your business online is that it might be a challenge to show your human side. People are not always interested in looking at plain websites. They might think that someone with an ordinary website is creating a list of products or services without being personal.

It is up to you to show your audience that you have a human side. With social media, you can express your views and feelings to others while assuring them that you care. You can give details about why your offer is special and how they can benefit from what you are marketing.

Express your human side when on social media and people will start to follow. They will want to see what you have to say and will love you for it. More importantly, it shows that you understand the needs people have. After all, businesses cannot afford to be depicted as massive smoke-churning factories that only care about profits. The businesses that care about people will remain strong and popular and most importantly, profitable.

The thing about showing your human side is that it makes people trust you. People don't trust corporations or generic websites, they trust real people. If there's any appropriate way for you to share your story, this can not only greatly increase people's respect and trust for you, but it can bond them emotionally to your company. This can mean they choose to patronize you instead of a competitor even if the competitor may have a bigger marketing budget or better prices or some other type of apparent advantage. We have to remember that consumers are often not rational and make emotional purchasing decisions. Anything you can do to connect emotionally and personally with your target market could have a big payoff.

Improved Brand Recognition

Marketing Consultancy, Digital Snazz says, "It is important for people to recognize your brand. Your brand reflects your business, its image, what you sell, and the values you hold. Your business will succeed when your brand becomes easier to spot. Using the right social media marketing strategies will make your brand visible and unique."

As you increase your social media reach and polish your image, it becomes easier for people to identify your brand and everything your brand means and signifies. You are showing people what you want to say and that you are vigilant and most importantly that you're a real and reputable business that is worthy of their hard-earned money and valuable time.

Your social media profile will include things like the logo

or name of your company, for starters. After that, you will post things on your page that illustrate what makes your work special and attractive. You can even talk about new developments in your business as they come along. You have full control over what you do on social media.

Another approach worth considering is posting information that isn't necessarily directly promoting your business, but more relevant information that you think your customers will find useful or informative. It's an indirect way of increasing the perceived value of what you have to say. Your customer will start to think everything you say is important and helpful if you always strive to provide them with quality information instead of trying to simply sell them something.

One example that illustrates this tactic is when hotel companies or travel websites have blogs that give travel tips. For example, a hotel might post a blog post about 10 of the most amazing things to do in their city. While some people may read this and not pay any attention to the hotel brand, there will certainly be those that will be interested in hearing what else the hotel company might have to say. If they feel the quality and value matches what they're looking for, this may be enough of a boost to induce to them to book with this hotel instead of a different one that isn't trying to actively help travelers with information.

In any case the more channels and avenues where people can find your brand, the more likely they will be to actually consider your offer and become loyal customers.

People who see your brand on different social media sites and hear from you regularly will be more interested in your offerings. They will note that you have something important to say. More importantly, people will have a clear understanding of what you present to them. They will know what your brand is all about and what your values are. Being recognized on social media is critical to your success.

Boost Your Brand Loyalty

Social media will help you improve your brand loyalty. By interacting with people on social media, your audience will start to become familiar with you and what you offer. Interacting with them and connecting with them is very important to building brand loyalty. They will be loyal to you—not just to your brand.

Loyalty is critical to the success of any business. You must have a strong customer base that will stick with you. Social media marketing makes it simpler to grow your business and make it more viable.

Anyone who follows you on social media will pay attention to your every word. Your followers will read everything you share and interact with you in many ways.

People want to hear you and see what you say. In particular, they will want to buy things from you, or hire your services.

Digital Snazz says, "Social media provides you with a captive audience that wants to hear about all you have to offer online." Everyone can learn about who you are and what your company stands for and why they should trust you with their business.. Your customer base sticks with you and hopefully will become lifelong followers.

Anyone who follows you on social media has access to everything you're doing as a business. All your updates will go onto their feeds, and keep them informed about everything you put forward. Letting people know what you offer is vital to your success even if you are just communicating with people already loyal to your work. It is more than just about getting money from those people. It is also to establish strong relationships so that they trust you and follow your messages.

Convert More People

This isn't simply about keeping in touch with existing customers, if anything its even more about getting new customers and growing your customer base. If you're not growing, you're dying.

Making conversions, especially online, isn't easy. It can be challenging to get people to recognize your brand and understand why it should be important to them. No one is going to take you seriously when you are just starting out. Particularly if you have no online footprint or followers that support you. However, with social media marketing, you will convert people quickly and effortlessly.

As you post things online through social media sites, people will want to listen to you and see what you offer. They will interact with you and read your blog posts, watch your videos, and so forth. You have to show people what makes your business stand out by appearing in the right places.

By humanizing your business, the conversions you require will be easier to attain. People like it when they see the emotions that a business wants to convey. There is also the benefit to interacting with people and answering questions, thus giving you extra help with getting your word out to more people. Don't forget about resolving any disputes or other issues people may have.

Getting onto social media is important as it helps you get onto more screens. When you learn to work with it, you will be successful converting people into being new customers that you can trust.

Generate more traffic:

Often, the end goal isn't simply to attract someone to your social media page or simply like your post, but what you really want is to get them to go to your website or store. One of the biggest goals of Social Media Marketing is increasing traffic to your website or e-store.

Digital Snazz say, "Promoting yourself on social media is essential. You can always post links to your site through a social media post. The link on your profile name or icon could go to your website too. Directions on how to get to a physical location that you might have could also be included. This could bring them to either your website or to the main profile page for your social media account."

People won't click on your link unless they think you have something valuable to say that is relevant to them and their interests. They want to feel appreciated and that their values or desires matter to you. For physical businesses, they will be intrigued by what you offer and will want to know your store's location.

Also, if your business employs affiliate links (for example a blog) the more traffic you can direct to your web page the more money you'll make. This is just another reason why getting traffic to your website is paramount.

You may have the best product in the world or the most amazing content on your website, but if no one can find it or if no one visits it, it's a complete waste.

Keep Your Marketing Costs Down

Generally, social media marketing is a lot cheaper than traditional advertising. You get more bang for your buck. It is often a challenge to conventionally market your business because it costs money to print ads, rent out spaces or spots in papers or websites.

By leveraging social media influence, you'll probably be able to save a lot of money. You will get your page marketed online.

Your presence will be interactive and inspiring to your audience. You'll be able to connect with them directly via messages and posts for free.

If you are smart, you don't need to spend a fortune on marketing. People will retweet, repost, or forward smart messages that you created. These messages will always include your name and a link to your social media profile. This makes it easier for you to market your work because other people are technically doing it for you.

Of course there are tools you should invest in, and all social media platforms have paid advertising options that are worth considering, but it's a mistake to rely on these paid forms of marketing. Although it may seem time-consuming to build an audience on social media, the payoff is much greater than paying for clicks on facebook ads. You have the chance to win the attention and patronage of a customer that may just become a life-long fan of your brand and may even become an advocate and ambassador of your brand to others.

Having people forward your messages is critical to your success. Even the smallest ideas can go viral in just a matter of hours. Just look online right now, and you will probably hear stories about some company or celebrity becoming the next big thing because of something that went viral on social media.

Get On a Search Engine

You will obtain more traffic from a search engine if your website has quality links and is Search Engine optimized. Of course you must make sure your content and links are unique and relevant to your original site and not just clickbait. The savvy consumer has become more and more discerning and suspicious of online content and they are less and less likely to fall for cheap tactics and clickbait so don't even bother trying. The goal here is to build something sustainable, not just make a quick buck.

Search engine optimization (SEO) is a very important when building an online presence. With this, you can link up to different valuable keywords. Use the right keywords to make your content optimized for all of the most important search engines.

What is also interesting is that your site will appear on a

search engine multiple times thanks to your social media channels. A Facebook channel will appear separately from your main website or an Instagram or YouTube channel, for instance. You can do this often as you want, but you must be aware of how each setup works. Although there are many SEO wizards out there that promise to make your site ranked on the first page, what many successful marketers are finding is that search engines like "google" are almost impossible to deceive. Google only wants to provide quality information to its visitors so rather than filling your site with irrelevant backlinks, focus on constantly generating quality content and Google will handle the rest.

In addition, your primary website will appear on search engines because proper links to social media pages are provided. Businesses with several social media accounts are more likely to appear on Google and other search engines than other groups. Often, blogs and social media posts and pages rank higher than the original websites in search engines. Therefore, if you can focus on generating more quality content than your competitor, over time your brand may rise above your competitor's in social media rankings.

The links between your social media sites and your main website are also important. Having more of these links ensures your main website will be easier for people to read and use. This is vital to your overall success as it helps your visibility on a quality search engine.

As you can see, the first step always must be identifying

your goals. This must come before identifying your approach. You can't come up with a process to reach your goal if you haven't defined what the goal is in the first place. For some extremely indepth strategies on how to get started with achieving these goals, see step 3.

Second Pillar: Finding Your Target Market

Equally as important as defining your goals is finding the right customer. So many businesses have started and failed not because their product was bad and not because their marketing was bad, but because they were going after the wrong customers. When marketing, remember to focus on your customer and their needs, not your product or service, or yourself. People don't care about you, or your perks. They care about how they can benefit from what you have. And you need to realize that your audience is intelligent. They don't want hype, they want truth. The more you hype, the more they'll be looking for the catch. So if you give them the honest catch right away, they'll stop looking for it, and they will begin to trust you.

Remember that until you've listened to what your customer has to say and understood what they are really looking for, you cannot have a real target market. You can't base your marketing strategy off your gut feeling, or your unproven belief that this particular type of customer will be interested in your product.

Give them the reality, the hard part of what you sell, the truth, and they won't have to look for it themselves. They can sit back, relax, and know the worst is on the table. They can simply focus on the good qualities, and all of the benefits your product can actually offer them. Then they'll honestly weigh the value added to them vs the "catch" or the drawbacks if any, and if you do your job selling the positive qualities honestly, and it's a product you believe in, it should be a no-brainer for them.

Realize that if you have a good product, you can simply tap into their interest. There should already be interest for it in your marketplace, so you simply tap into that interest. You don't need to try and create it by overhyping. Give a clear presentation of the benefits and what's in it for them, honestly.

Then, hand them the catch.

Marketing Copy and Pitches:

Keep your "me, I, my, our, and mine's" to a minimum, and instead focus your marketing approach on "you and your's." If you've written out your marketing pitch, or you've scripted it, check how many times you use "I, My, Our, or Mine" and compare it to how many times you use, "You," and "Your's." The latter should far outweigh the former.

Make sure that you speak to an individual rather than an audience. People want to feel like you're talking to them directly. The really smart marketer speaks to ONE Person.

One version is a speech, talking to an audience. You all, some of you, many of you, all of you...

And the other version is a conversation. People are much more willing to be invested in a conversation than in a presentation.

Building a brand is all about building trust. The more you can build up a relationship with people and things that they can relate to you on, they can trust you more. The more they trust you the more they're willing to come back and the more they're willing to spend their resources with you to improve themselves.

When you make videos or write a book, make sure that you are talking to one person and one person only. Direct your wording and your focus to a single audience member. It can be someone you know, or someone you envision. But do not address any group of people. Do not make it about many, make it about one person. This will make your customer feel like they have a personal relationship with you and thus they will be much more likely to listen to what you have to say, buy what you're offering, and become a repeat customer.

Third Pillar: Optimizing Your Website to Achieve Your Goals:

Identify And Create The Keyword Strategy

What about when the customer is looking for you instead of the other way around? Your social media approach and your website optimization need to be designed with this question in mind. You need to be easy to find. People should be able to find you by searching one word or phrase. That is what a keyword does. A keyword is essentially a word, or a phrase, that a person searches for in social networking platforms and search engines such as Google, Facebook, Twitter, LinkedIn, and YouTube. You have to know what keywords people will be searching for and incorporate them into your website. Then when they type the word in, and click search, they will find your page. This will mean that you are doing it right, but it is not as simple as it sounds. In this chapter, we will see how to identify these words and how you can incorporate them into your marketing strategy.

Why Should You Build a Keyword Strategy?

There are many consumers all over the world who are

looking for businesses on search engines. They use a lot of effort to search for these businesses. But how do they do it? They use keywords. You, as a business owner, can use this to your advantage. You will need to ensure that your website revolves around the keywords that are in line with your line of business, and the words that your potential consumers may use. Think about it, in a sea of thousands, won't your customers be interested in looking for you in a straightforward manner? Or will they fancy using a complicated technique to look for you? They will obviously pick the former and you must help them in the process.

Keywords will help your customers and potential customers find you online. And that is not an exaggeration! You will benefit from it greatly and will see how your business goes from being small to being one that will cater to many people.

You may wonder how you can zero in on the keywords that are most common to your line of business. But there are techniques you can use to determine these keywords. However, you will need to be able to determine their popularity and competitiveness. Therefore, you must conduct tests and analyses to understand how effective various keywords are in attracting your potential consumers to your website.

This section will help you learn how to define keywords, which will in turn maximize the potential to draw prospective customers into your business through different social networks. You have to make use of the best words that will help them find you. The research to identify the best keywords is an ongoing process, and the best words and phrases can change with trends and you must make the effort to follow this closely. You will be able to gather valuable information on the trends of the industry, and the demand and supply of various products. If you conduct thorough research on keywords, you will be able to avoid spending extra money on different packages that help you advertise your products. You will also be able to improve the traffic to your website.

How to Build Your Keyword Strategy

When you wish to start out with keywords, you should have a set strategy in mind so that it becomes easy for you to repeat the process.

This section provides you with the basic strategy that you can follow to build your set of keywords.

Identify a Minimum of Three Keywords

Think of your business from a customer's perspective. If you are a small business, you cannot expect your potential customers to know the name of your company. If you are a large business, you do not have to worry about the first keyword. However, you will need to come up with a list of words or phrases that define your business or your product as a whole. This will give you your list of three or more keywords. Since this is the very first step of the process, you must start out on the right foot. Do as much research on the topic as possible before you go about the process. See what other companies are doing and go about it the same way.

Identify the Keywords Based on Relevance

There are certain keywords that you may zero in on in the above step, but you should check their relevance to your business and also the level of difficulty. There are many words, like "marketing" or "business" that are very competitive. These words are difficult to rank in results produced by search engines.

If you are a small business, you should choose words that do not exhibit too much competition. These words must also be related to your business. (This goes back to the importance of finding your niche market and differentiating yourself). These words are often known as the long tail keywords. A keyword that has a great amount of search on it is a competitive word.

So, trying to use these will mean that you are trying to compete with several people. That might slow you down or make the process more difficult for you. There are different tools that you can use to identify the competitiveness of keywords that you have settled on. This will also help you identify new words that you can use to benefit your business. The most common tools are the Google Keyword Tool and the HubSpot's Suggest Keywords.

The other important factor about choosing your keyword is the relevance of that keyword to your business. There are some keywords that are difficult to rank. But these words may or may not be relevant to your business. You can do a small search on Google and check words that are popular in your category. You must strike a balance between the relevance of the keywords to your business and their level of difficulty. From the list that you create above, you should choose five keywords that match your business best. If you do not have that many, brainstorm and identify some more. You can always try new keywords to see which fits your business best. After all, it's not an exact science. Most people achieve the right balance through trial and error.

LSI – Latent Semantic Indexing

Your website will appear on a search engine results page (SERP) only with the help of keywords. These primary keywords give an idea as to what your website is really about and when a searcher searches for those particular keywords, your website will pop up on the results page. To make your website more relevant, you can use LSI keywords. It is a method by which search engines determine whether your website has good content and is on-topic or if it is just spam.

Most people understand LSI keywords, or long tail keywords, as they are known, as mere synonyms for primary keywords. This might be true to an extent but it LSI keywords are more than that.

For example, let us take the term "teacher." This is a primary keyword but there are a million other websites, which use that keyword. LSI helps in making an educated guess by using the rest of the content and deciding what type of teacher is actually being discussed here. If your website makes use of terms like "keyboard," "music," "notes," etc., your website will appear in searches related to music teachers. Search engines know that words like "chord," "bass," "alto," etc., and other words closely related to music will appear in a good article. These jargon words are known as LSI terms.

When a searcher starts a search, the search engine reads your article and determines the keyword density by looking at the entire number of words in the article and finding out how many times particular words or phrases are repeated in the article. Words that are often repeated have a higher keyword density. Including these keywords in the title, first paragraph, and last paragraph of your article will help increase the keyword density, as the search engines put extra emphasis on these areas of the article. It then picks out the words with the highest keyword density and decides what the article is about. The search engine has a database of related terms of any keyword and if those related terms do not appear, it is given a lower relevancy score and is placed below others. Articles with higher relevancy scores will rank higher in the search engine's results page. Repeating the same phrases will not help but using synonyms can make a difference and give the reader content that is richer and legitimate.

Design Your Website Around These Keywords

Once you have narrowed down the list of your keywords to five, you then have to incorporate these keywords into your website. The main focus of this activity is to enable your website to be found. For this, you should make use of these words in the best possible way. You will find out how to do this in the next step.

Optimize Your Website

You have made the list of keywords that you need to use for your business. You now must ensure that you increase the ranking of those keywords to enhance the chance of attracting people to your website. Search engine optimization (SEO) is your savior!

If you want to get web traffic, you will need to aim at being at the top, or somewhere on the first page of search results. If your potential customers are not satisfied with what they find in the first few posts, then they will quickly move on to the next few. And if you happen to be there, chances are they will visit you and like what you have on offer there. So don't underestimate the value of two or three spots below the first result. Once you land there, you can slowly climb higher and higher. The top spot is a coveted one, as most people select their choice from the first page of results. This spot is what all companies, big or small, are after. If this is not possible, you need to aim at being in the first few pages, say the first five, of the search. How many times have you moved to the second or third page when you haven't found whatever you were looking for? So, it will pay to make that effort and try to land on any one of the first five pages. Additionally, Google has advised most businesses to design their websites for their visitors, or potential customers, instead of for search engines. You need to keep this in mind in order to do well in the market. But before that, you will need to learn and understand what SEO is, and how it can help you optimize your website and search.

What Is SEO?

SEO is an acronym for search engine optimization, which means optimizing your website to help you land the first spot or one of the first five spots in search results. There are two types of SEO; on–page SEO and off–page SEO. On–page SEO refers to the way in which you present your words on a search engine. You can work on improving this immediately, if necessary. Off–page SEO is a reflection of how strong your website is on the Internet. This is determined by what people on other websites say about your website. This is something that may take time to improve. Although on–page SEO only affects 25% of the ranking of your website, it is best to start off with this, since it can be improved very quickly. Let us work on improving on–page SEO for your company.

The Main Elements of On–Page SEO

Regardless of whether you are already making use of this or not, this segment will look at some of the main elements of on-page SEO.

Since this is the easiest to clean up, you will learn how to do this. The steps that follow will help you identify what you must do. This section covers seven elements that play a major role in helping your website rise to the top of the search results on any search engine, or social networking platform.

The Page Title

This is a very important part of the website. This is like the title of a book. Consider this for an example – you are walking past a bookstore and decide to walk into the store. You have the urge to walk up to the fiction aisle and look for a book that is worth reading. Would you pick a book that has the worst title possible? You would not. It is the same when it comes to your website.

The page title is seen at the top of the browser window when you visit a page. When you are creating a page, the first option that you have is to create the page title. So, make this your first step before proceeding to the next one. The titles of the pages also appear in search engine results. You will find the page title in the HTML file for your website. The text of the page title will be in between the "<title>" and "</title>" tags. You need to ensure that you make your page title very effective. Here's how you can do it:

-       Formulate a sentence that incorporates all the keywords that you came up with earlier.

-       Make sure that the title is no more than 70 characters in length. This is because no search engine has results with long page titles in them. If you make the title too long, you will be reducing the importance of the keywords in your title.

-       Try to ensure that the keywords are at the

beginning of the page title. They should be within the first few words in the sentence.

-        Ensure that the title has a font that allows the viewers to read what you have written. Some of the best ones include Ariel and Georgia. Don't worry if your website does not use these; you can use them just for your SEO.

-        Ensure that the name of your company is found at the end of the page title. But if you are a big brand, you can avoid this since most people will look for the pages on your website using your brand name.

-        Try to ensure that you use a different title for each page. This will help you target the different keywords that you have listed.

Once you add the title, you will be given a permalink to the title. You can either choose the suggested permalink, or change it to your liking. This permalink is what will be the link to the page on your website.

The Meta Description

Meta data is a feature that can help you attract many more visitors. These viewers will frequently view your website if you have meta data. It does not affect your ranking on a social network, but it is good to ensure that you have a few of your keywords mentioned in the meta description.

What is meta data? It is the text that is seen right below the link to your website provided by any search engine. This description is what will attract viewers to click the link to reach your website; however, this will only happen if there are keywords to be found in the meta description.

It is like reading the gist of what is to come. Try to condense it to tell the reader what is in store. It is similar to what is written below a headline in a newspaper to expand the idea of the headline.

You should realize that the meta description is not found directly on your website; instead, it is just a summary of your website for search engines. If you do not include the meta description while coding the website, you will find that search engines just use information that is found on the page. This information is shown to viewers. The meta description is not understood well by most people and this is where you, as the owner of a business, may be making a mistake. So understand the difference and make the most of this feature. You will soon notice that your website will be much more discoverable, and that there is more scope for your website to show up higher on search engines.

The Headings

When you see a piece of text that appears larger than other text on the page, it is most probably a heading. This can be verified easily. You can view the HTML code of your website and check if the text comes between the tags <h1> and </h1>, <h2> and </h2>, or <h3> and </h3>. If you do not know how to do this, you can ask a developer to help you. In fact, it might be necessary for you to get professional help, as making a mistake can cause the headline to look bad.

The text in the headings is the part that is always read by search engines. Search engines assume that the text in the heading contains the keywords and it will ignore the rest of the text on the page. It is for this very reason that you will need to include keywords in the headings. It is best to use the <h1> tag, since that provides the largest font and has the most weight. There are other tags that you can use to enhance the view of your page, like <h4>, <h5>, <h6>, and <h7> tags. However, it is advisable not to use them since they do not have the same effect that the <h1>, <h2>, and the <h3> tags in your source code do. The other tags dilute the importance of the keywords that you use in them.

Cascading Style Sheets

Your website looks the way it does because of the code in your HTML. The HTML code is the back end to your website. It is the code that any search engine reads. The search engines extract the information that it finds relevant to a given search.

The cascading style sheet, or CSS, is what provides the layout of a given page in your website. This enables you to define how the headings and other elements in your page look. You have to use CSS for all your pages. However, you have to avoid using this information, which helps you enhance the layout of your page, in the HTML code of your page since your search engine may use that information.

Images

When you were three years old, you loved the storybooks that had a lot of pictures included in them. This is the same when it comes to a website. Images always help in enhancing the experience of the users. You must also be well aware of the adage that a picture is worth a thousand words. The same applies to your website, where images will help you get noticed better. When you are working on the code of your website, you can try to use images that will describe your website. Again, if you are not aware of how to go about this, then make use of a developer. Make sure that you keep the following points in mind:

1.   Do not use too many images on your page. This will make your page slow to load. This has a negative impact on viewers, since most of them are impatient, and will leave the website if it doesn't open fast enough. They won't want to wait for a page to load. They may choose to move to another page immediately.

2.   When you have pictures on your page, try to insert text describing your pictures. Whether it is your product or a service, you need to describe it effectively. This is important since most search engines do not read images. They are generally only comfortable with reading text. Search engines may miss out on some important keywords if they are only found in the images, and not in the text. Try to separate the keywords using a hyphen or a dash (-).

The Domain Info

You will find that websites that have been on the Internet for longer have a better ranking when compared to newer websites. This is because the length of time a domain is registered indicates the commitment of the owner. So when you start off, you must decide to stay with the same name and not change it from time to time. Try to remain loyal to the domain. Websites with short domain names may be considered spam.

The Google Crawl Date

Google crawls through websites very often and updates the information that it displays to viewers. The information that it updates is mostly keywords and other SEO information. You have to ensure that Google crawls through your website often. This can be done only if you produce new content on your website. If you have a blog, try posting stories on it on a regular basis, since that will help to ensure that Google crawls through the post. If you are busy, try collaborating with someone and ask them to add something as a guest post. Similarly, keep updating your website from time to time. Add something new like a product image or a description. All of this will ensure that Google crawls through your website.

Avoid Keyword Stuffing

You have read a lot about how important it is to ensure that you include keywords in your title, headings, and so on. You may believe that the more keywords you have the better your rank will be. You may begin filling your page up with all the keywords that you can think of. Please do not do that!

If you fill up your page with keywords, it may end up looking like a word salad and this will not interest visitors. This could also be viewed as a way of cheating search engines, which is bad thing to do. There are detectors that will ensure that you are not trying to trick search engines into believing that your page is good. If you are caught trying to trick them, search engines will usually leave your website out, leading to absolutely no publicity. The idea is to sprinkle keywords here and there and make it aesthetically pleasing. It should be like a well-peppered dish, which tastes much better than something full of pepper that is not mixed in well. So exercise caution and steer clear of using too many keywords in your description. It will end up being a big goof up!

Cookies

Have you come across popups like the following when you are using the net?

"This website uses cookies to improve user experience. By using our website, you consent to our cookies in accordance with our cookie policy."

You can make use of these cookies in your business venture too. First, let us start with the basics. Let us learn about cookies.

A cookie is information that a site saves to your computer using your browser. There are millions who use the

Internet every day. How can you keep track of all your consumers and frequent visitors? Cookies are the answer. Cookies tag individual computers so you'll know who is on your website. It is a non-invasive way to gather information about your visitors and their behavior. Obviously you will not be able to get all the information about your visitors. Educating yourself on what types of consumers are most active on your website and what their habits are will help you re-center and refocus your marketing efforts on the groups of people most likely to be responsive. Again, this is not an exact science and it will take testing and trial and error, but over time, you should be able to build a profile of your customer.

Cookie profiling or web profiling is having cookies provide basic information about your consumer's preferences. For example, if your website provides its contents in various languages, the visitor may select Spanish. If you used cookies, his language preference would have been stored in the cookie, resulting in faster and more convenient access by giving him the website in Spanish when he comes back. Basically, it creates a log of your visitors, stores their information, and applies the stored information the next time your website is accessed. The cookie file consists of the name of the server it was sent from, the lifetime of the cookie (if it is a persistent cookie) and a randomly generated number. This number becomes the visitor's computer's identity. So every time the visitor uses the computer to access your website, the server reads the number and remembers the visitor's preferences. If your website requires login, then these cookies will certainly help as it would have stored the username.

Cookies are of two types:

•   Session cookies

•   Persistent cookies.

Session cookies are temporary cookies that are created for temporary purposes and are active only for that particular session. When the visitor leaves the site, the cookie gets deleted. If you use such cookies, it treats everyone as a new visitor even though they have visited your website earlier.

Persistent cookies are also known as permanent cookies; the name speaks for itself. This type of cookie remains in the visitor's browser and gets re-activated when s/he comes back to your website. These cookies are the ones that remember your visitor's preferences. These permanent cookies also have expiry dates on them and they delete themselves once the expiry date arrives. When a regular visitor comes back, a new permanent cookie will be generated.

Imagine walking into your favorite restaurant and being greeted personally; the waitress already knows what you like, so she brings your usual order. How would you feel? Like you're at home? This is the same feeling that the visitors get when you use the cookies properly and give them a tailor-made experience. This will definitely keep your customers loyal and also bring in new visitors.

Of course you cannot depend on cookies fully, as many people do not like their online activity to be monitored and thus block or delete cookies.

Content Marketing:

There are many platforms that have made it easy for a person to publish content on the Internet. You have been able to develop a good understanding of the importance of keywords and how you can identify a list of those very words. You have also learned how important it is to ensure that your webpages and content are optimized for social media and search engine results.

The next step is to understand how you can ensure that more customers view your website through content marketing: blogging or posting content in different forms. How many times have you seen blog posts and articles in your news feed? I'm sure you have often visited a particular website after looking at the content. Adding a blog to your website can greatly increase your traffic and visibility. However, there are also simpler ways to create content. You could begin creating content for eBooks, or by taking part in various conversations that happen on the Internet, such as on Twitter or Facebook. This will help you to make sure that as many people as possible are discovering your business and exploring it.

Blogging is the best solution, at least to start with, because not only is it easy, but it is effective when it comes to reaching as many people as possible! Let us look at the things that you must consider when you wish to start a blog.

How to Think About Different Business Strategies

When you are blogging, you need to stop thinking of yourself as the owner of a business, and start thinking of yourself as a publisher of a magazine. As a publisher, you have to publish articles that not only promote the business but also share information about the industry. This should be done as it would be done in a regular industry.

You have to turn into your own public relations officer to ensure that people are seeing your stories the way you want them to.

You have to think about what you are writing about and the kind of words that you are using. You should never use terms or shop talk that only people from your industry or the employees in your company would understand. Your aim is to publicize your company and you have to do whatever is in your power to show it in the best light. Don't take this step lightly, as it is your best chance at promoting your business effectively. When you were brainstorming for keywords, you thought about the different words your customers would use when they were describing your business. You will need to use those keywords in your blog posts, or any other posts that you are writing on your business. The second and third chapters of this book should have helped you understand the importance of the kind of words that you use.

Setting Up a Blog

It is important for you to gather content that your potential customers will find interesting. However, you will also need to find a way to put that content is online. There are many tools that will help you publish it online. Be sure that you select the perfect platform for blogging. You will need to keep the following things in mind:

1.   The blog that you are starting should be part of your business's website. You need to realize that your website without a blog is like a regular brochure. A brochure never changes. You do not want your business website to look like that. They should have many connections and should be interlinked to each other.

2.   Add new content to the blog on a regular basis. Search engines award higher rankings to those websites that have new content added consistently. You must update it from time to time and also have others contribute towards it. You will see how doing so will help your blog to stay "trending" and also increase your customer base. These higher rankings help you gain more consumers for your products and services.

It is important that your blogging software is easy to use. But it is even more important that the content that you create for your blog is interesting. Avoid making it monotonous. You will regret having wasted an opportunity where you could have used your power to increase your reach.

There are quite a few blogging platforms that are easy to use and help you make your experience easier. These platforms have content management systems, which help you enter content with ease without having to worry about the coding. You will be able to edit information on the website without waiting for a developer to enter your content onto the page. If you are unable to find the ideal platform, then you must ask around and look for the best webhost for your blog. You can make use of Wordpress, as it is the world's number one content management system.

The Key Components of Your Blog

As was mentioned earlier, it is important for you to study the different components of a topic if you wish to understand it thoroughly. In this segment, we will look at the key components of a blog.

There are many components that a blog must have and it is essential that you have this in order to gather more attention from your potential customers.

A Title that Grabs the Attention of the Reader

It is your blog title that people will first lay their eyes on. You should ensure that this title is the frosting on your cake. You should use the correct keywords and make the title concise so that it grabs the attention of your readers. Only when it has the keywords that they are looking for will it pop up on their screen. Try to keep it customer-oriented. That means that you must know your target audience in order to understand exactly what they like to read. It is like decoding their mindset and supplying them with something that will help them remain interested in what you are trying to say to them. It will help to do your research and ask people in your target age range about the keywords that they would look for in a blog.

Text that Is Well-Written

Once you have got your title, you should work on the content of your blog. Let us assume once again that you are in a bookstore. You have picked up a book with an interesting title and you begin reading. You read the first few pages and find that the book is very boring. In addition, the author does not come to the point even by the end of the book. Would you recommend such a book to a friend? It is the same when it comes to blogs. The article that you write must be precise and it must be formatted so that it is easy to read. You can break the content into different headings and paragraphs. More importantly, you should write well and make sure that there are no errors. Keep it as interesting for your reader as possible, and don't fall into the trap of writing content that is not to your readers' taste. That will defeat the whole purpose of writing the blog and you will end up disappointed.

Use Images and Videos

As mentioned in the previous chapter, it is always good to use images. There are times when they speak louder and more clearly than words. Let us assume that you are talking about an event where a thousand trees are planted in a dry patch of land. It is better if you have pictures to back up the text. It is even better to make sure that you follow up on that story and continue to show the growth of those plants. If you use images, you are breaking up the text into fragments, which makes the article more pleasing to the reader's eye. Similarly, you can make use of videos that are in keeping with your blog. Ideally, they should be professional photos that are clear and of good quality. This will make the blog more relatable and believable.

Include Links in Your Article

When you are writing about something that has become famous all over the world, it is best to insert links. You are probably familiar with the term back-linking but, in case you are not, it refers to adding links to different sites in your blog. These links should all lead to different pages on your website. For example: If you are talking about a theory that has been developed recently, you cannot expect every person to be familiar with it. Therefore, it helps to insert a link to the content you are writing about. You can also insert links to your own website or to landing pages, which will help you gather more views to your content. This is discussed in detail in Chapter 6.

Be Organized:

Not only should your content on you blog be organized visually, but also logically. People LOVE listicles (list articles). They like them because they are organized and it breaks the information down into steps that they can follow. It helps them know what the most important takeaways from your article are. For example, people will be more likely to read a travel blog post that's titled "The 10 Best Restaurants in Paris for Under $20," than an article that's titled, "Eating at Restaurants in Paris." If you can find ways to organize your content, people will be more interested and responsive.

Does your blog have a niche?

If you have a business and have started a blog, it is for a reason. But what is this reason? Do you want educate the industry and your potential customers about your products? No? You will need to educate them on the happenings of the industry. You want them to learn about the problems that they, as potential customers, may face in the market. You must also tell them how your product helps them. Many people make the mistake of talking only about their products and its features, and fail to discuss why the product is a good fit for the customer. You must avoid making this mistake and touch on the topic. You have to tell them what benefits the product will give them and why they must choose it.

You can start blogging by answering ten basic questions that you think your customers may ask you. Then you can begin your blog by answering the most important question. You can make use of a FAQ system to ask and answer the various questions. However, you can only choose the questions if you put yourself in the shoes of your potential customers. Try to work on answering one question per week for the next ten weeks. This will help you create a great foundation for your blog and go a long way to ensure that your blog is successful.

Once you are done with answering these questions, you can work on different ways to make your blog interesting. For example:

- You can write about different products

- You can write about the happenings in your industry.

- You can write about changes that have been made to your products.

Make sure that you include images and that the content in your blog speaks volumes for your expertise. You do not want to have content that does not reflect your knowledge. Try to avoid making technical errors. Don't take your audience's intelligence for granted. If you provide them with redundant information, then it will be useless. You also have to show your potential customers that you are passionate about what you do. This can only be done when you write from your heart. But keep the business in the back of your mind when you are working on the content for your blog.

Fourth Pillar: Finding the Right Platforms for your Brand

Throughout this guide, we will look into various options for social media sites that are useful for your marketing needs. You will become an expert on the various social media platforms and which of them might be most effective for your business. This can also vary depending on what your marketing goals are for a particular campaign. For example, if your goal is brand recognition one platform might be better, if your goal is brand loyalty, you might take a different approach with a different platform. Etc.

Naturally, you can always work with all social media sites we list here; as many as you want to make yourself visible. Nevertheless, that does not mean every single one of them is sensible for your needs, let alone easy to use.

Every social media site is different based on whom it targets and how it is organized. Each social media site is unique. Choose carefully when planning your social media campaign. If anything, having multiple social media sites is best as it gives you the opportunity to accomplish more.

This chapter looks into individual social media sites and how you should evaluate them.

Look at the main goals you have for a social media campaign.

Decide why you are choosing social media in the first place. Maybe you want people to be more aware of your brand. Perhaps you are just trying to get more leads. Perhaps you might be trying to get people to download an app or reach your physical place of business.

The social media space you visit should be chosen based on what your goals are. Facebook is ideal if you want people to be more aware of your work. LinkedIn is perfect if you want to get leads. Snapchat is ideal if you want people to download an app.

Whatever the case, look at what you can get out of a social media site before you start working with it. See that the campaign is arranged correctly and that you have a clear understanding what social media sites are perfect for it. You should carefully examine how individual options might work with your various needs.

Consider the target audience you are trying to reach.

Every social media site has its own specific audience. LinkedIn has a great platform that is popular among professionals, especially those who earn good wages. Instagram is useful for younger people and is prominent among today's millennials.

In 2015, the Pew Research Center found some interesting demographics surrounding social media sites. While this information is not definitive, it provides an idea of what to expect from certain social media sites:

• Facebook's user-base is extremely diverse. People of all kinds use Facebook - from the rich and poor to the young and old alike. It is equally popular among men and women and among black, white, Hispanic, and Asian audiences and other racial demographics.

• Women are more interested in using Pinterest. People from suburban areas are also interested in it more than others.

• LinkedIn is not only popular with wealthier people but also with those who have college degrees. People living in urban areas tend to use LinkedIn more often too.

• Younger people are more likely to use Twitter. Those living in urban areas will use it more often as well.

This is just a sampling of what you will discover about

social media sites. All of these sites are different in how they attract various types of people. Experiment with different social media pages so you can potentially get something meaningful and important out of your campaign. As you will discover, be watchful how you can use multiple options for your campaign.

Look at how often people might interact with social media sites.

All social media sites have different standards of how often people interact with them. Facebook, Twitter, and Instagram are the most popular places where people are more likely to check every day or every other day. Meanwhile, Pinterest and LinkedIn are places where people will check on their feeds three to five times a week although some might do that more often.

A site that has people checking it often if you are trying to increase your brand recognition might be advisable. Sites where people do not check their profiles every day are good if you are trying to get leads or establish long-term connections with professionals in a field.

Knowing how people behave on social media sites is important when you want to interact with them. Make sure you find out how well and how easy you can communicate with someone on a site. This is to make it easier for you to interact with people and to share your interests.

Review what your competitors are doing.

Your competition will more than likely be on social media already or contemplating joining in the future. Whatever the case might be, look at what your competitors are doing.

Check the websites of your challengers to see what others are doing. Be sure to do what you can to compete with them and of course make sure your approach focuses on your competitive edge and what you offer that your competitors do not offer. Doing so makes it easier for your page to stand out and be more attractive. Monitor the performance of your campaign and continuously tweak and adjust until you feel that your message is clear and well received. It's also important to make sure you are not copying whatever other people are doing. Using the same social media sites and working with similar keywords or other posting strategies is good so long as your content is original.

You do not necessarily have to duplicate everything your opponents do. Be aware of what someone else is implementing so you have a clear idea of what you should do yourself. Keep your mind open throughout the process, but at least examine the accomplishments of others.

Think about the content you want to create.

Every social media site is different in terms of the message you work with. You can do anything on a social media page, but you need to discover what the standards are for each site:

• Tumblr, Pinterest, Snapchat, and Instagram are great if you are trying to market things with pictures. These social media sites are perfect for pictorial-based marketing.

• LinkedIn is ideal if you want to be more technical. The site is also great for people who want to share their opinions with others.

• YouTube and Snapchat are good for video content.

• Quora is appealing if you want to answer questions that people might have about a certain concept your business has.

• Twitter is useful for when you want to share news or ideas with people. Although only if you are trying to share smaller bits of data at a time.

Review the context before you choose a certain social media site. This is all about getting some control over your work and having everything laid out in a smart and valuable manner. As you practice, you'll improve your ability to do this and your customers will catch on.

Look at the format of your content.

All social media sites have standards for how the content is posted. YouTube obviously focuses on videos while

Instagram is about pictures. Twitter is for smaller messages while Facebook and LinkedIn allow more details about what you want to post.

Decide on what to post and how it will be illustrated. This is to give you a better approach to handle your work.

Think about the subject you will utilize as well. Some businesses might work better with specific types of content. A tax preparation firm might do best with blog posts explaining changes in tax laws, for instance. A baseball training facility could benefit from having video posts showing people learning how to play the game or honing their skills.

Be careful when launching your campaigns:

Don't run too many social media campaigns. Know how well you can handle individual ones without getting overwhelmed. While you can work with as many social media sites as you want, only commit to what you are comfortable with handling at any given time. You do not want to forget about individual sites. In this respect, quality is more important than quantity. It's better to have one excellent campaign than 5 mediocre ones. Moreover, your customer will be annoyed if they are constantly being plagues by mediocre ads and campaigns. They will lose interest in your brand.

You can always use the analytical features from many

social media sites to see what is happening with your pages. Analytics examine how many visitors reach your site or interact with your posts. You can use analytics to assess the progress of paid campaigns you operate. This research will help you determine whether to stay with a particular platform or if you are better off elsewhere. Do not use anything too complicated or hard to follow because after all, your workload will get more difficult.

If needed, there is also the option to network with others in your business to work with different campaigns. You could hire one person to run a Facebook campaign while another works on LinkedIn, for instance. See how well those people handle individual campaigns and if they understand how certain social media platforms work. Allow multiple people to work with several channels at a time if you have to, but see that they understand what they are working with. The key is to keep everything in your social media campaign consistent and under control.

Remember that all the points introduced in this chapter are mere suggestions. You could always work with any of the social media sites you are reading about in this guide. Consider what each of these sites has to offer so you can do more with your work.

Now we will discuss in depth some of the most common social media platforms.

Facebook Marketing

There's no question that Facebook is the biggest social media platform in the world. If you don't believe me, consider these statistics culled from statisticbrain.com as 20 September 2015:

- Total number of monthly active Facebook users: 1,440,000,000

- -Total number of mobile Facebook users: 874,000,000

- -Increase in Facebook users from 2014 to 2015: 12 %

- -Total number of minutes spent on Facebook each month: 640,000,000

- -Percent of all Facebook users who log on in any given day: 48 %

- -Average time spent on Facebook per visit: 18 minutes

- -Total number of Facebook pages: 74,200,000

Any objections? I rest my case.

However way you put it, the above-mentioned figures

represent a LOT of people! And naturally, where there are many people, there are many prospects. And guess what? More prospects equal more business opportunities! Additionally, Facebook offers tremendous diversity, featuring potential customers of all ages, backgrounds, and lifestyle choices, enabling you to reach your target market successfully. No matter who you are trying to reach or what you are trying to sell, you can find the appropriate clients on Facebook.

Why It Makes Sense

Of course, we're not saying all 1 billion+ users are your actual prospects or potential customers. Many of the active Facebook members will be far from the market you are seeking. But what such the statistics imply is that in terms of exposure, there's no better place on the Internet for marketing than Facebook. But this is just the tip of the so-called social media marketing iceberg. Let's take a look at other reasons why marketing on Facebook makes so much sense.

Segments

Here's a very interesting piece of useful information: Facebook keeps a vast database on just about everything and anything related to its users. Favorite things, location, age, likes, interests and more... check! So what's the point?

There are two ways to advertise your products and services on Facebook: free and paid. The information available in Facebook's database is particularly useful for paid advertising. Why is that so?

Traditional advertising like radio, TV or print ads uses a shotgun approach – i.e., mass advertising where you simply hope there's enough of your target audience to watch, hear or read your advertisement. But with Facebook, you have the ability to target specific market for your paid advertisements.

For example, your business is an Italian restaurant located in Nebraska. Further, yours is a rather eccentric one that plans to cater specifically to people who love Italian food and who worship the late David Bowie. You can advertise your restaurant on Facebook and filter your advertisements to target users who live in Nebraska, who love David Bowie and worship Italian food. But considering Nebraska's quite a large area, you can further narrow down your target audience to those living in Norfolk!

Another example – say you're a freelance author who specializes in personal finance. You can market your e-books on Facebook using paid advertisements to target people between the ages of 20 to 30 years who are interested in learning how to invest for their future. If you're rather chauvinistic and would like to limit it to male audiences, you can instruct Facebook to show your advertisements to men only and maybe even further, you want to only reach men between ages 20 and 30 with a college degree.

Facebook can zero in on any niche no matter how small--which is not even remotely possible with traditional media. It is this specificity that enables social media marketing to shine in ways previously unheard of. By targeting the exact demographic you are looking for, all the way down to interests and location, you are securing the best possible odds of increasing your sales exponentially and enabling your business to develop in ways once impossible. The other great thing about these filters on facebook is that facebook will tell you roughly how big their potential population is with all your filters in place. This can help you determine if your niche is the right size. Too many filters may mean your niche is too small and there aren't enough people to reach, without enough filters, your niche is too large and you'll have too much competition to deliver an effective message.

Cost Management

You can easily limit your advertising spending when conducting Facebook marketing campaigns. This is because you can control not just the maximum amount you're willing to spend for such campaigns but also how long such campaigns will last and how much of your budget to spend every day.

For example, you only have a maximum budget of $30 for a 30-day Facebook marketing ad campaign. Facebook will automatically limit your spending to $1 per day over the next 30 days to keep you within your budget. As such, you don't have to worry about runaway spending. This enables you to start with advertising within your reach, no matter where your business is financially and expand your marketing campaigns when and if you have the ability and desire without having to stress about the money invested in it.

MARKETING ON FACEBOOK

If you want to maximize your market reach as well as Facebook's features, you'll need to understand some of the best Facebook marketing practices. While these aren't necessarily hard and fast rules, following these practices can significantly improve your product or service's ability to engage customers on Facebook.

And remember what I kept saying earlier: Social media marketing is primarily about engagement. If you go out and study the Facebook pages of many of the world's most popular brands, one thing you'll notice is that they hardly ever sell directly to followers nor do they preach to them. Instead, they engage.

These days, consumers are much more savvy and wary

of sales pitches on the internet. They can usually tell if you're just trying to sell to them or if you're sincerely and genuinely engaging them. Always keep in mind that Facebook is a social network first and foremost, and it's not a sales and marketing network. People want friendliness, respect, and inclusion- they are on Facebook to socialize and to have fun, not to repeatedly listen to and ultimately reject ill-advised sales pitches. Engage them, involve them, and they will reward you for it. Give them a generic advertisement and watch your prospects fizzle. The choice here is clear.

Think of the way you use Facebook: you get on it for entertainment, to connect with friends, and to get information. You don't go on Facebook to get out your credit card and shop. Thus, you have to approach marketing on Facebook subtly with a hands-off approach.

Thomas Meloche and Perry Marshall, in their book Ultimate Guide to Facebook Advertising, discussed how different Facebook marketing is from traditional advertising, whether it's online or on print, by using a front porch story or analogy, which goes something like this:

Imagine that you live in the middle of a town square. Imagine further that your house features a front porch where you enjoy watching people pass by. On the porch you're cultivating many beautiful plants. There days when you're enjoying watching people pass by and drinking from a pitcher of cold lemonade that some of those people notice your front porch's beautiful plants and approach you to ask how you keep them looking beautiful.

You offer them seats on your porch and give them glasses of cold lemonade while explaining the general principles for keeping your plants beautiful and healthy. Some of those people become so interested in plant cultivation because of your sharing that they'd be willing to spend money just to have a day with you and learn the finer details of how you grow and keep plants beautiful. You take them up on their offer and spend the next day teaching them how you do it.

In that example, did you observe any explicit or direct attempts to sell anything on your porch? How about any implicit attempts to promote a horticulture seminar? That's right, none! And in a nutshell, that's how you do Facebook marketing. Any selling is done only within the framework of relationships and personal connections.

As I always say, it's about engagement. A good way for you to engage people on Facebook is by posting helpful tips or links to articles that they'll like and share as well as by asking relevant questions. When your posts focus on your audience, their needs, and their interests, you develop relationships, which is the single biggest reason for the existence of social media. People want to view you as one of their friends. It pays to talk to them accordingly. Helpful tips on things they might want or need is great, upselling them things is not. Focus on your customer's happiness over your own success, and you'll wind up fulfilling both goals. And as the preceding porch story has shown, sales can be a result of just such relationships.

Another great way to engage your prospects and customers on Facebook is by consistently posting unique and quality content every day. Although it may seem quite cumbersome to do it at such frequency because of very busy schedules, posting such content less frequently increases the risk that your target audience may miss some of your important posts. This is because over time, they tend to follow and like more and more Facebook pages.

And these "new" likes and follows will compete for their social media attention and engagement. When they miss more of your posts and see more of others', their interest in yours starts to dwindle and in others to increase – and there goes your prospects and sales leads. If you are short on time, keep in mind that such posts don't have to be long. Aim to make them eye catching and interesting. Try to include content that stands out amid a sea of other posts, no matter how daunting that may seem. Keep in mind the interests of your target audience- your posts certainly won't sway everyone on Facebook, but they don't have to for you to succeed. Catch and hold the attention of the customers you want with attentive engagement and quality posts and you'll have loyal clients for as long as you maintain your activity.

Several studies recommend posting 3 to 5 times daily on Facebook for optimal engagement with prospects and customers. However, every situation is different and as such, I recommend that you employ sensible and strategic experimentation to see which will work best for your business. Make a goal that works for you, be it once a day or ten times daily. Just aim to be consistent and post regularly to keep people looking forward to seeing what you have to say.

Lastly, you should keep your posts fun and interesting. Remember, a big chunk of successful engagement is having fun so keep your posts helpful, interesting and light as much as possible. No one wants to be overwhelmed with heavy, difficult content in their free time. Informative entertainment, ideally with pictures, videos, or other visually compelling additions makes for an ideal goal that will catch and hold the attention of your target market, leading to eventual conversions.

LinkedIn Marketing

A social media site specifically created for business communities, LinkedIn's goal is to give its registered members the opportunities to build and establish documented professional networks of people that they know and trust. LinkedIn personal profile pages prioritize or highlight work experience or history and education – 2 of the most important criterion by which people are evaluated in the business world for business partnerships or employment. The profile page also features a professional network news feed with several modules that can be customized.

Basically, membership is free, and members are referred to as "connections". Another basic difference between LinkedIn and social networking platforms like Facebook – aside from its business theme – is that LinkedIn requires that you have a pre-existing relationship with a prospective connection first before being connected. Many aspects of LinkedIn, including that one, are designed with a more professional, business oriented mindset than most other social networking sites, including Facebook, can boast, though of course that leads to less of the light-hearted social interactions that Facebook is full of. LinkedIn can be a valuable resource for connecting you with other businesses or with business professionals, and can be an ideal platform for targeting anyone within that demographic.

LinkedIn also offers several premium account options that give you more unlimited usage of the platform. Additionally, you get more insight into business trends and industry info that you may not have been aware of. Also in the premium accounts, you can send "InMail," which is a direct messaging system that allows you to send targeted messages and promotions to recipients of your choice.

SOCIAL MEDIA MARKETING, LINKEDIN STYLE

Because this is all about building networks, what you're actually marketing on LinkedIn is yourself as an entrepreneur or business professional. Obviously, the more you market yourself professionally, the more business contacts you gain, which is only beneficial for your businesses in general.

So how do you market yourself well in LinkedIn? One way is to build up your profile of course! Since you're selling yourself, make yourself look good. LinkedIn isn't just about being sociable and engaging- major aspects of most other social networking sites. Here you can sell yourself, and your business, so don't be too shy or modest about your strengths. You can build your profile up in LinkedIn using the following features, as well as others:

-Status Updates: Short statements about you that you think your connections will find most interesting or useful. Here, you can include content-related links to other sites, including your business's own, as well as links to other relevant sites and your other social media accounts. Posting actionable and useful status updates regularly can make you look more active on LinkedIn. Activity will show motivation and work ethic and will go a long ways towards showing prospective connections how dedicated and professional you can be.

-Blog Posts: This site lets you effortlessly syndicate your profile with your blog posts and vice versa. What this means is you can allow your LinkedIn profile to update automatically with your blogs on your business' website by providing a link and abstract of such blogs.

-Presentations: You can also post slide presentations such as those of Google Docs, PowerPoint or SlideShare to your LinkedIn profile.

-Events: You can post events on your LinkedIn profile to promote events that you're either promoting, managing or conducting.

-Tweets: You can also connect your Twitter tweets to your LinkedIn status updates to better keep your connections and followers updated on your latest happenings.

You can also brand your LinkedIn address by customizing it. Much like a personal website, a branded

LinkedIn address can help boost your professional image. Choose wisely—the address you select will represent your company. You'll want to appear professional and select something well suited to what your business sells, offers, or represents.

Lastly, you can use LinkedIn's Community Features to collaborate and communicate with other LinkedIn users. These include Groups, Answers, and Company Pages. Groups keep you informed and in touch with other LinkedIn users of the same interests and passion. You can either join an existing one already or create your own!

The best way to expand your social (and business) circles is to add great value to discussions when you participate. Keep in mind, you are still communicating as a business and the persona you created for that business. In discussions, you will, of course, want to appear personable and friendly—but on a platform like LinkedIn, there is room for greater formality and professionalism than you might present on alternative networks such as Twitter or Facebook.

Answers is an excellent way to connect with similar-minded colleagues as well as share your expertise with others, promoting your profile – and business – indirectly. You can connect by asking pressing and intelligent questions and let other experts chip in their advice and in the process, connect with them. You can also toot your own horn (not too obvious, though) by answering questions as an expert too.

Both methods are a valuable way to form additional

connections and to show off your intellect and thoughtfulness, provided you do so in a humble, honest way. Both asking and answering eloquently worded and reasonable questions can earn you the respect of other businesses and individuals you will encounter on LinkedIn.

Lastly, you can use LinkedIn's Company Pages to look for business partner companies as well as spy on competing ones. This can help you determine the most effective marketing strategies to use, as it allows you to consider markets your competitors have not yet tapped. It also enables you to take inspiration from their current or previous campaigns, (of course you should be modifying them to make them your own), or may prompt you to explore new territories where your competitors may not have a dominating presence or advantage.

Further, you can set up a page for your own business where you can show your expertise in your industry or niche and indirectly promote your company or business. Here, you can publish key information about your business such as website address, business address, and company or business description. Be sure to be thorough and accurate in your descriptions.

Google+ Marketing

Google+ focuses on joining and creating communities, where you can share links, blog posts, and other content promoting your business, as well as allowing you to view and discuss the content shared by others. Like with most social media platforms, it is very important to engage with and communicate with your future customers. Throwing a bunch of links promoting your business at them will feel too impersonal. But once you gain their trust, it can make for a comfortable place in which to interact with customers and share business links, promotions, and thoughtful or interesting posts.

Naturally, depending on the nature of the community or communities you start or join, you will want to customize your posts and contributions to suit your audience. You would do well to join a number of communities to maximize your success with Google+. After all, even within your target market, you will encounter diverse people with varying interests- learning what they are likely to enjoy and become a contributing member of those communities will enable you to gain the most conversions. You can reuse the same link in each community, provided it is fitting, but make sure you customize your comments to the community so that your links and content make sense and are appropriately personalized.

Google+ really shines with it comes to SEO. Getting

comments, shares, and plus ones on your contributions on Google+ works wonders when it comes to getting your website ranked highly in search engines, not least among them Google itself. And let's face it, where's the first place everyone starts when they have a question or are looking for information: that's right! Google! Due to the obvious affiliation of Google and Google+, Google creates a back-link to articles, websites, and other content you contribute, generating additional SEO hits for your company.

Over time, you can even gain an Authority rank, which comes from having a large community circle with lots of activity, both yours and others in reference to you. In essence, it enables you to gain a higher ranking because you have a superior online reputation, plus it grants you an increased rating when determining who ranks highest in search engine optimization results. This is not an easy rank to come by, of course, but investing time into Google+ to accomplish it can reap significant results for your business.

Another important thing to note about Google+ is that through Google Hangouts, you'll be linked to Youtube, enabling you to pair perfectly using Google+ and Youtube seamlessly. This increases your search engine results across both platforms, particularly if you are ever inclined to include some live video streams, which have a number of benefits. They rank higher in search engine optimization results than traditional methods of filming the video prior to posting. They also truly demonstrate your charisma and competence to your customers, as well as increase their trust and respect for you since it is much, much harder to fake or hide things while live screening a video.

Be warned that Google will track your activity. This can be a blessing or a curse depending on what you make of it, but if you use it will, it can be a fantastic platform to select due to its Youtube collaboration and its propensity to rank you highly in search engine optimization results.

Instagram Marketing

As you may already know by now, Instagram is a social media website which lets its users edit, filter and share pictures and videos to many other people over the Internet. It also allows users to simultaneously share these over Twitter, Facebook, Flickr and Tumblr. According to statisticbrain.com, Instagram has over 183 million registered users who have already shared more than 18 billion pictures and videos that garner an average of 1.65 billion likes daily as of 11 September 2015. If that's not big enough for you, I don't know what is!

Businesses have also started looking to Instagram to sell their brands, particularly because pictures (and videos) paint a thousand (and more) words, and our brains think better in pictures. These major businesses include G.E., Adidas, Virgin America, American Express, Intel and Red Bull, among many others. In reality, almost every major business out there has some type of Instagram presence, but many do not take full advantage of the platform or execute a good marketing strategy with Instagram.

Intel, for example, promotes their latest, cutting-edge processors via Instagram with pictures of the latest computer models that utilize them. More than just posting pictures on

Instagram, they post highly creative pictures that make their otherwise "boring" products come to life with excitement. It features all sorts of technological wonders on its Instagram, including both widely available products as well as more eccentric but rapidly growing choices like 3-D printers. Its Instagram account features a wide range of photos that paint different pictures as to how Intel's products continue to influence our way of life as we know it.

In contrast, the Instagram account of Virgin America is less creatively styled than most others. At one point, they used photos of the very popular Pomeranian puppy Boo in promoting their first class flights as dog-friendly over this social media site.

American Express promotes its financial services on Instagram, particularly by posting mostly photos of the many important events they've sponsored as well as by using #hashtags in promoting their products' image as those that are essential for modern living.

Keep in mind that while you can post short videos on Instagram, it's not optimal to do so. If you're gunning for video promotions, your best bet is still YouTube, which is designed primarily for uploading videos. Focus your resources on beautifully creative pictures and images on Instagram to optimize your use of this particular social media platform.

Posting pics on Instagram isn't as easy as snapping photos and uploading them – at least not for social media marketing purposes. Before you promote your products or services of this social media platform, consider your target audience, the optimal engagement strategy and what will provoke them into talking about your brand and photographs. When you know your audience well, you'll know the kinds of pictures that'll appeal to them. Instagram allows you to get truly creative with your marketing, enabling you to use it to advertise virtually any product. Once you get to know your customer base, design a beautifully well-pictured marketing campaign that will appeal to the audience you are trying to attract. When you know your audience well, you'll also be able to develop strategies that will get them to talk about your brand, which provides opportunities for engagement and consequently, brand awareness and promotion.

BEST PRACTICES

By also posting pictures of the people behind your products and services on Instagram, you "humanize" your business by allowing your followers to see the hands and faces behind the inanimate objects they are following on Instagram. Social media in all of its many forms depends, primarily, on connecting with our fellow human beings. Let your potential customers see you as you work, and witness the hands-on, emotional, relatable side of your business, as opposed to just the end result they so commonly see. Humanizing your products and services allows your followers to connect with your business on a deeper level and increases their chances of becoming hot leads and eventually, customers.

You can also draw in more prospects and leads by featuring pictures that show how your products are created and packaged or how your services are rendered. The point of doing this is to make your followers more familiar with your brand so they can become leads and customers. If they understand more of how your process works from the start, they are more likely to trust and rely on your products and in doing so, they will come to rely on your business as well.

Most people are naturally curious and knowing what goes into the creation of items they enjoy can make them feel more attached to such items, as well as offering them reassurance that the methods you claim to use are every bit as ethical as you suggest, gaining you additional trust and loyalty. Just don't give too much "detail" to prevent your competition from spying on you and undercutting you.

Lastly, use original unique and catchy #hashtags, Instagram's most effective marketing tactic. Using good hashtags can help your brand become more visible to more people, which can lead to more prospects, leads and consequently sales. You want a good mix of unique hashtags with more popular hashtags. To evaluate the popularity of a particular hashtag, all you have to do is type it into the search box on Instagram and you'll see how many other posts are currently using that same hashtag.

Youtube Marketing

Google owns this platform that allows its users to upload, share, comment on and watch videos. Its search engine is probably the 2nd biggest in the world next to its parent company and by far, the biggest video sharing website on the planet. As such, it's the best social media platform to use videos in promoting your products and services. But with so many videos being uploaded on YouTube – about 72 hours' worth of video every minute being uploaded on the site – how can you effectively reach your target audiences?

The first thing you'll need to do is create your own "channel" on YouTube, which should neither be too difficult nor complicated. Next, comes the most challenging part, producing very compelling videos for upload.

So what makes for compelling videos? First, consider the content, which should engage your target customers within 15 seconds or less. Otherwise, your viewers will be bored and won't bother watching your videos long enough to appreciate it. This is because of the information overload they're all subject to each and every day. To really engage them within the first 15 seconds, use introductions that are animated and quick to both spark their curiosity and win their trust. This helps them expect something great from watching the video further.

Another important quality your videos need to have are calls to action – and this is key for any social media campaign to succeed. You can place the call to action at any point on the video, depending of course on its message. Just ensure you don't overdo your calls to action because for one, having too many such calls may confuse the viewers or it may come across as aggressive or pushy. After all, much like Facebook, people are not on youtube to buy things. They're there to either find information or else be entertained. So you need to make sure whatever content you provide checks one or both of those boxes (hopefully both).

Some of the common and sensible calls to action you can consider including in your videos are subscribing to your YouTube channel, commenting on your videos, liking-adding-sharing your videos and visiting your brand's official website and/or other social media platforms, among others. These are less aggressive asks. This doesn't cost the viewer anything and if they feel connected to you and inspired by your content, they may well want to support you or at least they want to hear more of what you have to say.

And more than just compelling, you should also post videos on YouTube regularly to increase your presence in YouTube and consequently, increase the number of your subscribers. One way to ensure regularity is to create shorter videos of a particular long-form content, i.e., divide one long topic or video into series of shorter videos. Instead of producing a "movie", create shorter episodes that are not only easier to watch and understand but also spark more curiosity and interest. It can help if you release each new segment on a designated day and time, and remain consistent.

Once you get people hooked on your channel, they'll be eagerly looking forward to watching your new video each time a new one is posted, and if you let them know when that will be, they'll incorporate your channel into part of their daily routine. Be careful to avoid sporadic or infrequent updates, though, or your followers are likely to grow bored and no longer anticipate content, leading to less loyalty and fewer customers. Be consistent, and make it entertaining, and your current clients will recommend your videos to their friends, likely via social media itself.

VIDEO VISIBILITY

No amount of consistency in terms of posting high-quality and interesting videos on YouTube will ever make up for lack of visibility. After all, what good are videos – however excellent the content – if viewers can't find them? While this is more about search engine optimization (SEO), which is a very complicated topic to discuss here, you can do the following to improve your videos' visibility and allow more people to view it.

One is carefully written titles. Make sure that your videos' titles include targeted keywords and that they're followed by a colon (:) for optimal visibility. An example of this is a video on how to self-publish your first e-book with a video title "Self-Publishing Success: A Beginner's Guide".

Next are your videos' descriptions, which you'll need to begin with a full URL. You'll also need to provide as many details about the video as possible without giving away its main attractions or points so that people will still want to watch it. In other words, enough details without spoilers.

Twitter Marketing

Based on a survey conducted by Ask Your Target Market, about 42% of people who use Twitter do so to follow companies or brands. And since you're a businessperson who is looking to market your business over social media, that's great news! Next only to Facebook, Twitter is the second largest social media site in terms of users with over 646 million users as of 25 September 2015, according to statisticbrain.com. It offers a tremendously diverse and far-reaching group of people you can market to, and unlike the users of Facebook, many Twitter users actually want to be marketed to. As such, Twitter can be another excellent social media platform to market your products or services.

Compared to Facebook, Twitter is considered to be a micro-blogging website, i.e., you can only post updates that are at most 140 characters long. Initially, this limit was intended to make it compatible with most mobile phones and text messaging services. Since then, it has evolved into a somewhat useful and practical feature for sending and receiving concise and quick information among many people. This might make you feel restrained, but there is a lot you can do to gain attention, and you can say more than you'd imagine in 140 characters.

Using Twitter can help you market your product or services over social media by:

-Developing productive relationships with bloggers and journalists for PR;

-Enhancing your industry expertise and thought leadership reputation;

-Promoting your product or service's upcoming activities or events;

-Helping you find out how people think and feel about your product or service;

-Engaging your product or service's customer base; and

-Growing your brand.

MARKETING ON TWITTER

You can use Twitter as a very powerful marketing tool to help direct more traffic to your business website, promote your business' activities and events, monitor economic activity and share your expertise. By inserting a link in your tweets, you drive people to your business website and promote any coupons or special offers, inform them of interesting developments on your product or service and provide them with access to very interesting and quality content. Fans may even re-tweet the things you share on Twitter if they find your content to be very good and unique. This multiplies or leverages the amount of traffic that can be directed to your business website and as such, you gain access to more marketing leads. You can gently and enthusiastically request that people take the time to retweet content they enjoyed, thus generating a higher amount of interest in your company and what you have to say, or, more precisely, what you have to tweet.

By using the "Connect" tab on your Twitter account, you can monitor your product or service's activities on Twitter. You can also do this by signing up for updates that are sent via email. Lastly, you can use software to get a closer look at all of your product or service's Twitter activities.

Word of mouth is one of the best ways to market a product or service. And testimonials are one of those ways that your business can be promoted by word of mouth. Think about it: how often do you ask friends or colleagues for recommendations. If someone you respect recommends something to you, all of the sudden you're much more inclined to opt for the recommended product instead of competing ones. Often, we are so overwhelmed with choices that a friend's recommendation is the only thing we have to go off of and so it makes the decision for us.

A very good way of collecting good testimonials for your product or service is by using Twitter's "Favorites" feature.

Such testimonials are significant social proof for your product or service and can help enhance the image of your product or service, making it more popular. People are inherently social creatures, and if something is popular and well liked, they usually want to try it out as well. The more clients you have that favorite your business, the more positive reviews you will effectively hold. That will raise your reputation in the eyes of any social media consumer.

Using this feature is as easy as 1-2-3. You just hover over any tweet in your stream and then a list of options will appear, from which you can click "Favorite". Your product or services get more social proof as the number of favorite tweets contained in your tab increases. It's well worth favoring tweets your followers and potential customers share as well, particularly any that support or reference your business or related businesses. It shows clients that you are listening and interacting with them, and it makes them feel special.

One way you can promote or market your business' promotional activities – like campaigns, webinars or events – is by tweeting about it and inserting a link that will direct people to your event's sign up page. It's best that you come up with a very nice hashtag for your activity first before you even tweet about it. Including diverse and descriptive hashtags will ensure your tweets are present in a number of different categories and increase their visibility. Inappropriate use of or simply lacking hashtags will lead to your tweets not getting much attention. So take advantage of this free promotional tool.

You can help make your brand a preferred or leading one by tweeting useful resources and tips regularly. As you do this, it's best to tweet a good amount of both your original or owned resources and those of other people's. Apart from establishing your product or service leadership, it can also project an image that's humble and open. This makes you appear personable-almost human, yet also knowledgeable. A source that people can trust and depend upon is a resource they'll happily utilize.

When using Twitter, keep in mind that there are a number of tools and programs that you can use to maximize the time you spend and to ensure you gain the greatest amount of followers. Many of these work by making it easier for you to find people and companies to follow- and it helps you to notice when someone you once took an interest in becomes inactive so that you can unfollow. It's worth noting, of course, that many of your clients will use these tools as well, so strive to ensure your own activity does not fall too low, lest you disappoint them.

Public Relations

Public relations is a very important part of any effective marketing campaign, traditional or modern (i.e., social media). One way to do this is by introducing your business and your products and services to those who can spread word about them far and wide – the media. Because many media people such as bloggers, reporters and journalists are also on Twitter, it only makes sense to use this micro-blogging site for effective public relations or PR.

One way to do this is by first following or subscribing to blogs that are most popular or well known in your particular industry or niche. From there, you can glean ideas as to which influential or beneficial Twitter authors or personalities would be best to follow. You can also follow well-known journalists who cover your industry or niche and tweet about their published works and get their opinions on industry or niche-related topics, which can help you get on their good side. Once you do, you can tweet them about your products or services, taking care not to "sell" them. Establishing such professionally personal relationships with influencers can go a long way in promoting your brands. In many cases, it will cost you nothing, and having powerful and influential friends like these effectively results in free advertising for you. Favorite and retweet what they say, get to know their thoughts and opinions on things, and your business will flourish as their endorsement will excite new potential customers into converting.

Pinterest Marketing

Pinterest, like Instagram, specializes in pictures and images. As such, in order to use it successfully, you must master the art of creatively putting your products and services into image form in a manner that catches the eye and entices your potential customers. Pinterest enables users to pin images that appeal to them to their Pinterest page. Each pin includes a link to an external site, such as that of your business. Pinterest works similarly to a search engine, where users can search for keywords or phrases to find applicable images that suit their fancy.

You might wonder whether you should choose Pinterest or Instagram considering the similarities. Pinterest can work very well at boosting your SEO sources and as such should be considered as an alternative or addition to Instagram. It will also depend on, of course, on the demographic you are looking to target. Both platforms boast high numbers of women, but Instagram features more teenagers while Pinterest usually markets itself to those with crafty or other creative interests and pursuits.

Those using Instagram usually are seeking personal experiences and unusual pictures, whereas on Pinterest individuals are seeking tips, tutorials, and inspiration, primarily. You can certainly utilize both resources, but tailor your content accordingly, or select the one that suits your product. Also, pinterest is quite popular with people looking for recipes and DIY home decorating and arts and crafts.

Pinterest enables you to create beautiful and spectacular themed boards, which are collections of pictures that can tell a story or pull at the heartstrings if assembled and ordered carefully. You can utilize this feature to represent a product or a promotion and to encourage people to pin images from your Pinterest board, raising further awareness of your business. You can pin images, articles, tips- anything informative, thought-provoking, helpful, or otherwise compelling, though be sure to select something that complements the goals of your business as well as inspiring your customers. As always, use hashtags appropriately to generate greater interest in your company's social media accounts.

Pinterest also enables you to gain the support and recognition of your current and future customers as well as the recognition of other businesses that you might want to work with by way of pinning content they post. Doing so links back to their page, and they might, in turn, support you as well, which can generate a substantial amount of increased traffic to your website.

If you put together creative, useful, and visually appealing Pinterest boards, it can be a great resource in getting more visits to your site, which can be particularly useful if you are just starting out and still trying to generate awareness. Instagram falls somewhat short here as very little will be linked back to your other sites and that can make it more challenging if you are still in the early stages of conjuring up customers at all.

Be warned, though- Pinterest will not show those interested in your pins everything you post. The platform recommends content for its users based on their interests, which it generates from things they've viewed and pinned over a period of time. As such, if your own contributions are not entirely consistent some of what you share might never be viewed by your prospective customers at all. If you are still unsure between Pinterest and Instagram, considering using LinkedIn to scrutinize the choices of your competitors. If they all seem to favor one over the other, it may very well suit your products and services better. That said, a pioneering attitude is not without its merits and if you embrace the less popular choice you might find an opportunity to shine.

With about 70 million users and unique opportunities to share curated content and generate vastly increased views of your other sites, Pinterest is a social media platform well worth considering, particularly if you are targeting young adult women as part of your intended demographic.

Tumblr Marketing

Tumblr is another primarily visual social media network with an ever-increasing amount of young users serving as its primary audience. You can include written works and articles on Tumblr, but its ideal use is best suited to pictures, animated GIFs, and videos, short films, or movies. Audio files are also getting increased attention on Tumblr and therefore might be a good area to potentially explore if your business lends itself to that type of content.

On Tumblr, a sound strategy to gain followers and attention is simply to follow others, preferably those within your target market. Tumblr does not display the number of people you are following, or, for that matter, the number of people who follow you. This enables you to safely get to know your audience and customize your own posts and content to suit their interests. It is even a platform that enables you to post, follow, or otherwise appreciate fan created content based on your products, services, or business- a flattering gesture demonstrating loyalty and spreading awareness for your company.

In this way, you can engage customers by getting them directly involved and effectively enable them to do some of your advertising for you. If you run contests for your followers to generate fan created content for you and offer a prize for the best creation, you will have an excellent promotion that is fun for everyone involved. I highly suggest letting the community vote on the best one in such competitions, making it an exciting experience even for those who do not directly participate. Any submissions can be used and appreciated in your own marketing campaigns, both on Tumblr and on other social media sites.

Like with Pinterest and Instagram, making things visually striking will really appeal to the Tumblr community. Unlike those two choices, however, hashtags are not an option on Tumblr, so you should include compelling keywords to get your posts and content noticed. Aim to feature eye-catching pieces that trigger an emotional response, or something humorous, and you are likely to go far on Tumblr.

Fourth Pillar: Keeping Your Brand Image Consistent

No matter what, your brand image is, it has to be consistent throughout your social media marketing campaign and especially across platforms. Social media enables you to project your brand to thousands if not millions of people either in your area or across the country, and the unique identity of your brand needs to be preserved.

The issue is that keeping your brand image consistent throughout your social media campaign is more difficult nowadays than it was in the past. When social media was in its infancy and business owners were just beginning to realize the benefits of marketing via social media, it was very simple to keep a consistent brand image throughout the marketing process. Today, although its more challenging to keep this consistency, it's arguably even more important now than ever.

Fortunately, there are some tips that you can follow to ensure that your brand image remains as consistent as possible throughout the marketing process. And when we say 'brand image,' we don't just mean the literal logo of your brand. We mean keeping your brand's look, underlying message or theme, and voice the same throughout the marketing process as well.

Let's find out how you can do this:

Make Sure the Look of Your Brand and Content Is Consistently Familiar

While all social networks operate differently or have a unique layout, that does not at all mean that the look or layout of your brand needs to change between social networks. In fact, the opposite is true.

For example, the colors and fonts that you use in your social media needs to remain consistent in your content. The biography of your company should be the same across all social media networks as well, while any brand images or profile images that you have need to remain the same too.

Make Sure Your Brand's Voice Is Consistent

Your brand's voice is not just the style that you use to speak on your content, it's how you interact with your audience. For example, is the voice of your brand witty and energetic, or down to earth and serious? Regardless of the style of your voice, you need to embody it everywhere: in the content that you post and share, in your blog posts, and in how you interact with users across all social media accounts. Doing so will solidify your social media presence and make people recognize you better.

Post Regularly... As in Daily

To ensure that your brand image remains consistent, you need to ensure that your posts are consistent as well. Posting consistently not only will provide more opportunities for users to engage with you, but it also allows you to develop what your voice and identity is. Maybe you have an idea of what you want it to be but you haven't put it to the test yet. Posting daily, at the minimum, allows you to experiment until you find the right brand voice that you need. Eventually, once you start posting daily, it will simply become a habit and that's good for ensuring that users are viewing new content every day.

Repurposing Content

When we say repurposing content, we simply mean that you take content that you've already posted and then find a new spin to put into it. For example, let's say that you've written a blog post two months ago that contains a lot of numbers and figures. You can now repurpose that content by converting the figures and numbers in the blog post into an easy to see chart that you can then post on your social media pages for users and followers to share.

Fifth Pillar: Tracking Your Competition

Don't forget that your competition is going to be using social media as part of their marketing strategy as well. Keep an eye on your major competitors and your developing ones and see what you can learn from them in regards to keywords and insight. If your competitors are successful in their social media marketing campaigns, identify what they are doing right and then brainstorm how you can do the same thing in a more innovative and appealing way.

By keeping track of your competition, you'll be able to unlock new opportunities while realizing past failures and doing what you can to avoid those failures. Either way, you'll gain much valuable new insight into social media marketing and find ways to outdo your competitors little by little.

Here are some things to look for when keeping track of your competition:

What Keywords Are Your Competitors Using?

Discovering what keywords your competitors are using can be time consuming and difficult, but by thoroughly analyzing their content and blog posts, you should be able to identify several keywords that are repeatedly coming up. If there are a lot of keywords that pop up continuously, it shows that they're doing something right.

Which Type of Content Is the Most Popular?

Of all the content that your competitors put out there, which of it is the most popular? In other words, what content of theirs is getting the most shares, is receiving the most likes or comments, and seems to be circulated around the internet the most?

Once you find the content that appears to be the most popular, you can determine what kind of content it is. Are videos, photos, or regular posts being shared the most? And what is the subject matter of that content that is repeatedly being shared? This will allow you to see what people tend to like the most in your niche market. Then, when embarking on your own social media campaign, focus on the same type of content that is proving to be the most popular with your competitors.

Monitor the Activity of Your Competitors

Monitor all of their social media accounts. Subscribe to them all, not just one or two. You should be aware of any new update that they make as soon as it comes out. This will give you much better insight into what they are sharing and what is proving to be the most successful. This will also help you understand what direction they're moving in as a company and help you plan your own efforts accordingly.

Also, monitor how often or how well your competitors respond to comments from users. Do they respond 24 hours after or just an hour after? Do they respond in a manner that is helpful or not? Do you see consistent complaints that you can capitalize on? For example if your product is a software and users of a competing software continually complain about glitches in the system, perhaps you can center a campaign around your glitch-free system. You won't directly mention your competitors, but customers who are frustrated with your competitors may see your message and consider switching to your brand.

Are there any links that your competitors link to, and if so, what are any patterns that you can spot in those links? Do they link to the same blog or site repeatedly, or different blogs and sites, for example:

Read The Blogs of Your Competitors

Finally, if your competitors are running any blogs, you need to be a regular reader of them. This is one of the best things you can do to come up with ideas for your own blog in a way that could surpass your competitors.

Check up on your competitors' blog(s) daily and read each of their posts thoroughly. Again, look for any keywords, patterns in their writing style, whether their posts are long and detailed or short and to the point, and what type of comments they receive from readers. If your competitor is running a successful blog, then you'll know what you need to do with your own.   But if your competitor is not running a successful blog, then all the same, you know what you don't need to do as well.

Sixth Pillar: Outsourcing and Time Management

The Time You Need Now

Time is the one commodity that you cannot buy, sell or trade, and yet it's the one thing everyone would love to have more of.

Far too often, the time you think you have is not your own. Traffic, meetings and a constant barrage of interruptions gobble up the time you thought you had in your schedule, often causing you to shift and refocus your day's activities. With only 24 hours in a day, most people find themselves eating while at work, taking tasks home, and even giving up sleep in order to maximize their time. The result is that they are less productive than ever.

The question is, how do you make the most of what you have?

If you've wanted to find a way to get a handle on your time, you're not alone. There are time management strategies that can help you be productive, accomplish your goals, and most importantly, control your schedule so that you have time to do everything you want.

Time management begins with priorities.

The lesson of the glass jar with rocks, pebbles and sand can help you understand how to prioritize the most important things in your life, as well as manage your time.

Maybe you've seen the presentation about how to manage your time. In the lesson, a professor displayed a single large glass jar. The jar represents your life.

Next, the professor took out a bag of large river rocks. He picked one up and held it up so that everyone could see its size. "This rock," he said, "like the many others similar to it, represents the huge things in your life. These are the things that you value more than anything, like your family, your goals, your health, and even your education."

The professor poured the river rocks into the jar. "Do you think the jar is full?" he asked. The class affirmed that it was.

Next, the professor held up a bag of pebbles for everyone to see. "These represent your career, hobbies, friends, and even your home," he said.

He poured the pebbles into the jar, and they filled up the spaces left by the big events in life represented by the river rocks.

"Is the jar full now?" asked the professor. The class was certain that it was.

"Not so fast," said the professor. "Next comes the little details, the minutia that can complicate your life if you let it. But when I pour this sand into the glass jar, it still will not be full." The sand poured into the jar and began to fill the gaps and spaces between the rocks and the pebbles.

Next, the professor added water to the jar. The class was convinced that there was room for nothing else. The jar was full.

"Wait!" said the professor. "There is always room for surprise and delight!"

With that, much to the enchantment of the students, he plopped a colorful fish into the jar. It was a reminder that even when your schedule is full to the brim, you can still make room to enjoy beauty and pleasure.

If the professor had filled up the jar with sand first, however, there would be no room left for the things that really mattered.

Effective time management strategies, like prioritizing what's important and what is not, can help you control both the important and the little things that take up time in your day. Time management strategies don't have to be difficult. Often they are fairly simple.

The hard part is doing them so you can get the time you

need now.

Why You Can't Get Anything Done

Have you ever had plenty of time to get something done, and found that you just couldn't meet your deadline?

Or maybe there's just too much on your calendar. Your schedule is overflowing; you have sticky notes on top of your sticky notes as reminders of everything that has to be done. And yet in spite of all of your good intentions, it's impossible to do what you set out to do.

There are plenty of reasons why that happens.

Distractions

We live in a world of distractions. With the onslaught of technology, our lives can appear every bit as busy as an urban metropolis that never sleeps and never turns off the lights.

Some distractions are unavoidable, but most we carry with us or intentionally seek out.

Perhaps the greatest distraction is the one we use for

business and entertainment. It never leaves our hands or our pockets. We give our mobile phones the power to hold our attention and keep us from what we should be doing. Although they can be a great tool, the mobile phone is a source of constant distraction because you can check social media and news, play music and games, and respond to digital and voice communications. It's often possible to engage in several of these activities simultaneously.

Your cell phone offers endless diversions, and it's the number one distraction today. Teachers don't want their students to have them in classes, cities prohibited drivers from using them while driving, and bosses despise seeing them in meeting.

Time-saving tip: Put your phone on silent mode when you're working on a task — that means no ring tone and no vibration. The sounds will tempt you to pick up the mobile device to peek at what's going on. You have voicemail on your phone, and you can set your email with an automated response. If need be, both of these mail devices can indicate that you will return messages within the hour.

Starting and Never Finishing

Follow-through is the difference between getting the job done and leaving it unfinished.

If you play golf, you know that to drive the golf ball where you want it to go, your swing determines the ball's direction and velocity. Once you commit just swinging the club, you have to follow through. You don't stop when the club makes contact with the ball you follow through to complete the drive.

Time management of your schedule is much the same. Think of the ball as the project you're working on. The swing is the work you are doing. Just because you made contact with your project and got it started, doesn't mean you can walk away just yet. You've got to follow through, just like the golf swing.

If you never finish the swing, or the project, your heart was never in it, or you didn't see the importance of the effort it would take to complete the task.

Emergencies

Emergencies will happen, especially when you least expect them. Not all emergencies can be prevented; however, you can be prepared for crisis before it happens.

Have a backup plan for those times you know you're going to have to miss lunch. That may mean having a stash of energy bars or other snacks in your desk drawer so that you're not emptying the vending machines of snacks. By being prepared, you don't have to worry about running out of fuel.

Sometimes other people have emergencies that will affect you. This happens frequently at doctors' offices. Patient emergencies requiring the doctor's immediate attention may delay your appointment and throw your schedule out of whack. To better manage time in the event of an unavoidable situation, take something with you that you can work on. For example, use the time to catch up on your reading or emails that need to be returned. You can shift your schedule around after your appointment.

Procrastination

Procrastination remains the largest annihilator of time management. Even if you're are a black belt at scheduling and planning and you keep your distractions to a minimum with Tiger-mom vigilance, there is still a chance you will lose all track of time thanks to procrastination.

Procrastination is the one thing that most people are good at, too. It's only natural to put it off what to put off until tomorrow what we ought to be doing today. You tell yourself, "I have plenty of time." Do that enough, and you will quickly find that you have run completely out of time and are now facing an impossible time crunch.

In a situation like this, one of two things will happen. Either you will finally find your focus and forge ahead to complete the project you're working on, or you will give it up entirely and work on something else.

If you choose the first path, you may find yourself going without sleep, eating junk food, and putting something else on the back burner until you have time to get to it. Giving up means that you have one more project you were not able to see to through completion. It may be that the project wasn't particularly important to you in the first place. You discovered that you have no passion for it.

Regardless of the reason you gave up, no one likes to be known for starting and not being able to finish a project. Your best bet is to take on fewer projects, manage your time better or stop taking on tasks for which you have no passion.

Strong time management skills can keep you on track and help you complete your projects on time.

You might be tempted to think that the more organized person is the better they are at time management. That's not always true. In fact, the most OCD people can find ways to self-sabotage their own time-management skills. They're too busy trying to make everything perfect. In seeking perfection, they too procrastinate, unable to let go of a job that is good enough.

So how do you get stuff done? No one strategy works for everyone, and many people use several strategies to focus find on what needs to be done and see it to completion.

Try some of these time-saving tips:

Make a to-do list

Sometimes the easiest way to manage time is to figure out what you need to spend your time on. The list can be a simple and efficient way of cataloging everything you need to get done. The nice thing is that as you complete each item on your list, you can check it off. By placing a tick next to each task, you can see the progress you're making. Success gives way to more success. Every time you check off one of the items, you know that you're making that much more progress.

There are those who say the list you live by is also the list that can kill you. That can be true if you write down every single thing you do in a day. Imagine if your to do list began with wake up, throw back the covers, swing legs out of bed, place feet on floor…. You would be spending so much time writing down the things on your list and checking them off that you would never accomplish anything significant.

In essence, you're focusing your time on the sand in your jar of life. You'll never get to the pebbles or the rocks that represent the more important things in your life.

Set a timer

Using a timer has been an invaluable tool for many people. It's unreasonable to think that you can commit yourself to eight interrupted hours of work. Even trying to commit to several uninterrupted hours can create fatigue. You may find yourself slowing down as you try to complete the task before you. Eventually you'll find yourself running out of steam.

Instead, set aside a predetermined amount of time. Within this timeframe allow for task completion and a short break. Work for the amount of time indicated, and then take your break. No fair forging ahead during break time. Get up from your chair, take a brief walk, step outside, get a glass of water or a cup of coffee, and come back to your desk and your next work segment re-energized and ready to go.

Some people find that they can work best in 80 minute increments followed by a 10-minute break. Others like a 45 or 60-minute period of work followed by a break.

One of the most successful time management techniques is the Pomodoro technique. The idea is to select a task and work on it for a period of 25 minutes. When the timer rings at 25 minutes, take a short break no longer than five minutes but no less than two minutes. After you have completed a set of four Pomodoros, allow yourself to take a longer break, anywhere from 15 to 30 minutes.

Using a timer can keep you focused on your tasks and give your mind the break it needs. You'll also learn how to effectively gauge how much you can accomplish in a designated period of time. And as a result, you'll be able to better plan your schedule.

Outsource Outsource Outsource:

If you take away one thing from this section, let it be this:

outsourcing can allow you to take your business to the next level. One of the biggest mistakes entrepreneurs and business owners make is that they think they have to do everything themselves. Or else, they think they need to be a big corporation with lots of money before they can have employees. Not only is this false, but this belief is keeping you from achieving success in your business.

Nowadays, with websites like Upwork and Fiverr, you have access to hundreds of thousands of freelancers in every industry under the sun. They're all competing for work to do and thus, prices are good because of competition, and quality is also good. Any aspect of your business that you can outsource—find a way to do it. If you're a business mind, you're probably not a graphic designer. Hire a freelancer to design stuff for your marketing campaigns, not only will the finished product look so much better, but you'll have saved yourself hours of effort and frustration. You can even hire Virtual Assistant and researchers to do all the brunt work for your marketing campaigns. If you need someone to do all the research and provide you with reports of what your competitors are doing or provide you with market intel, you can have it for a great price. If you need someone to handle your company's social media accounts and follow up with every comment and every follow and unfollow, you can easily hire a virtual assistant to do this.

What this does, is it allows you to focus all your time on growing the business. You will be free to think bigger. Instead of having to do every tedious detail yourself, you'll be able to simply direct others, trust that the work will be getting done, and then think bigger. Think about the next thing. Only allow yourself to work on things that you really excel at—outsource everything else. Think about things that only you can do in the business and outsource everything else. If you don't take advantage of the outsourcing and freelancing revolution that is happening under your nose, your company will only grow at a snail's pace or simply die all together.

Seventh Pillar: Value First, Money Later

Why do you think even your folks and grand-folks are on social media, particularly Facebook? Well, it's because it's a lot of fun being there! There has never been a time such as this - thanks to social media - where anyone can connect with so many people, express themselves in ways and magnitudes never before available, and get so much affirmation (or hate, as the case may be). And in many cases, such a great privilege gets abused or used irresponsibly.

If the possible repercussions for you personally can be undesirable when you use your personal social media account irresponsibly, think about how much more the undesirable effects might be on your brand or business if you handle social media in ways that can make you cringe. That being said, here are some basic principles that, if followed, will help you not just to avoid negative repercussions on your brand but also to maximize its sales.

Talk Like an Egyptian

Seriously speaking, what I mean to say by this is to post like a person - like what you would naturally do on your personal account. Now let me clarify this. I'm not saying post on your business or brand's social media accounts without filtering your content and just post how you feel like posting.

What I mean by posting like a person is don't post in a very business-like or stiff manner. In other words, make your well-crafted content sound conversational instead of corporate or like a presentation. Instead of writing "Evaluate the key features of Brand X at your most convenient time," you can word it something like this: "Hi friends! Go check out our latest product's features as soon as you can!" Doesn't that sound much more personal?

Another way you can make your brand's promotional content more personal or engaging is to replace technical product specs or features with benefits such products and specs provide. If you're selling a car, for example, don't focus on identifying its key technical features like "Euro-4 compliant engine" but instead, say its benefit like "a powerful yet environmentally friendly and fuel-efficient engine that can get you to your destination faster for less fuel."

In And Out

There are two types of marketing - inbound and outbound. Inbound marketing is about luring buyers in towards your business via advertisements or social media content. You sell to them after they've come to you. Outbound marketing refers to actively going to where your prospects are and selling the product to them, as is the case with telephone and email marketers.

When it comes to social media marketing, complement your mostly inbound marketing with some type of outbound marketing, like follow up messages via social media or email (if they joined your email list). Considering you can do it for free with a potentially huge return, i.e., additional sales, it'd do you good to use your brand's social media accounts to not just draw customers in but to pursue them as well. Just remember not to be pushy or aggressive, meaning it'd be best to follow up on prospects who have already responded to your inbound social media marketing in one way or another rather than hound people who've never heard of your brand before.

Content Is King

The key to effective social media marketing is engagement, i.e., getting people to take action on your brand's social media content whether it's in the form of "likes," comments, or shares/reposts. And obviously, the most important type of engagement is conversion or sales! If your brand already has a website, don't be complacent and think that's enough. Why?

You see, website traffic is only as good as the engagement they provide. The challenge with engaging people through your website is that it's practically impossible to engage them through it because, for the most part, business websites are static, i.e., aren't able to respond or interact with prospects and customers as quickly (if at all) as social media. Websites are great for lead generation, no doubt about it. But even the hottest of leads can grow cold if you don't engage them enough. Adding a social media component to your marketing efforts, regardless if online or offline, will allow your brand to engage people more effectively and hopefully, make more people patronize your brand through purchases.

Now, your brand's social media account - even your brand's website - won't be able to provide the engagement needed to sell if you populate it with boring, impersonal content. Without quality and engaging content, people will neither have a reason to engage with your brand nor follow it on social media. No engagement, no sales. Period.

Tell Them What You Want, What You Really Really Want!

No - I categorically deny being a Spice Girls fan. It's just that I have a thing for very catchy pop songs. And it just so happens that the song Wannabe's just so freaking catchy. And what better way to call this section of the chapter than by one of its most recognizable lines.

Okay, what I really meant to say in this section is this: don't forget to include a call to action on your brand's social media content. And what is a call to action? It's telling them in no unclear terms what you'd want them to do with regards to your posted content. Some of the most common calls to action in social media that you may have already encountered frequently include:

–Click subscribe;

–Follow us on Facebook/Twitter/Instagram;

–Like us on Facebook;

–Click "like"; and

–Click here to know more.

Often, social media audiences are clueless as to how to react to posts or are too busy to think about it. By including a call-to-action, you can remind them or give them an idea of the things they can do for your brand that you or your brand will appreciate. And when they act on your call to action, you increase your brand's social media engagement and consequently, its chances of closing more sales.

It Goes Both Ways

At its core, social media marketing is about a relationship between your brand and its customers and prospects. And the best way to evaluate whether such a relationship exists is by directly engaging with your prospects and customers. And relationships - genuine ones at least - are two-way, i.e., both parties communicate to each other. One way communication doesn't count as engagement because frankly speaking; there's no reciprocal interaction there.

One of the best ways to practice 2-way communications on your social media accounts is by acknowledging your audience or followers' positive comments. You can do this by commenting back with a thank you. Another way is by affirming their comments on your posts by writing something like "We know, right?" or "Spot on!"

The most crucial two-way communications can happen when somebody posts something critical or negative about your brand on its social media account. Never react to it with the same spirit, emotion and tone of writing in which negative comments are posted. Instead, take the high road by first acknowledging their concern by saying something like "I'm sorry to hear that" or "I can imagine why you feel that way." By acknowledging, you won't be validating their critical or negative comments about your brand or post. You'll just be telling them that you're not dismissing the way they feel or are saying that their comments are as logical as eating soil on a hot summer day. And in many cases, bashers are disarmed when they hear (or read) that their comments weren't easily dismissed or when they see that their opinions were validated, though not necessarily accepted as true or accurate. Doing so also shows your audience that your brand is classy and professional.

Step 8: Constantly Change

This is an industry and a time where technology is moving at the speed of light. So don't get comfortable. One of the biggest mistake marketing departments in big companies make is that they get too comfortable. Their current approach is working so why change it? That's great until the day comes when that current approach stops working—and it will stop working. Why? Because the times change, people change, and the world changes.

So, your marketing approach should change with it. If you're not constantly looking ahead to the next thing your business will surely die out. That's why it's SO vitally important to stay abreast of trends in all forms of media (social and traditional). Read the headlines, do the research, spot the trends and adapt your marketing approach accordingly. You cannot market in a vacuum. You're marketing to real people in a real world, so your approach must reflect that. If people were advertising things the way they did in your grandparent's day, people today would have no interest.

This is not to say that there aren't unchanging rules and guidelines to follow. There are, but your content and approach must change as quickly as the trends do. That said, we are including some general guidelines that you should follow regardless of changes in trends.

Posting Frequency

Think about how frequently you'll post content on your brand's social media accounts. Is it 3, 4 or 5 times weekly? It's important to determine this from the onset so you can already plot your content posting schedule on your calendar. If you don't, chances are high that you'll forget to post regularly on your brand's social media accounts, which can significantly affect its ability to consistently engage its audiences.

Your posting frequency can also be very helpful in terms of subdividing relatively large chunks of content into smaller ones, i.e., create a series of posts about it. Doing so can make it much easier for you to come up with engaging content.

General Themes

Having a general theme or topic in mind for your brand, product, or service can greatly reduce the need to brainstorm and think about what topics future content will be about. Take for example the website https://sunbrightcouple.com. The page's about living a beautiful life even during very challenging situations or seasons. The people behind it have identified several key aspects of life that contribute to one's ability to live a beautiful life regardless: relationships, income, health, and preparing for the future. Knowing their main theme and their sub-themes, content planning becomes very easy for them because they already know the kinds of content they'll create or share (other people's content) on their website and Facebook page (facebook.com/sunbrightcouple/) so they no longer have to brainstorm about what content they'll post. All they have to concern themselves with is to create or look for other people's content to feature on their Facebook page.

Automation

Finally, automation solves the challenge of not having "enough time" to post regularly due to busy schedules. There are apps on the Internet that you can use to automatically post pre-determined or selected content on your brand's social media accounts at your pre-determined times. Through such apps, you can just schedule about an hour every week to create or look for content to post on your brand's social media account for the whole week or month, program it on the app, set it, and forget it. The app will automatically post those content on your brand's social media sites. Examples of these apps are Agora Pulse and Hootsuite.

Bonus (Crowdfunding)

What is Crowdfunding?

Small business directory Manta sent a poll to its readers before a webinar on crowdfunding. One of the questions was, "Have you ever or would you consider crowdfunding as a source of funds?"

Less than 3% of respondents answered that they had used crowdfunding in the past and less than 15% answered that they would consider raising funds from the new form of financing. Asked why they would not consider crowdfunding, many business owners responded that they didn't want to be seen as needy by customers, or have customers think that their business was in trouble.

Given the rapid rise of crowdfunding over the years to 2015, this widespread misconception of the funding source really set us back. There are a lot of myths about crowdfunding. Besides the idea that it is only for those in need, most think of it as simply another source of financing.

Joseph Hogue says in his book, Step By Step Crowdfunding, "Raising money through one of the many online platforms can take your business to the next level but it is not the biggest benefit to crowdfunding. Crowdfunding is really about building a sense of community around a product or idea. It is about crowdsourcing your passion and building a crowd around your business."

Jamie Roy says in his Crowdfunding Recipe for Success, "Crowdfunding has been on the trending list ever since it attained public acclaim a couple of years ago. And why shouldn't it be? It has made investing in start-ups and small businesses more accessible to the common person." This is likely why crowdfunding is all the rage amongst people at all levels and age groups. The booming market for crowdfunding promotion services justifies just how big of a deal crowdfunding actually is.

However, crowdfunding has been shrouded with some debates in the past. A number of people don't consider Crowdfunding to be practical. In fact, some would even go as far as to say that crowdfunding can be used to exploit and con people of their money. While there are some risks associated with crowdfunding, the advantages it offers people with a vision are unparalleled.

Before you learn more about this subject, it's imperative to start with the basics. A lot of people don't understand what crowdfunding actually is and that can stop them from leveraging its perks. So here's a concise meaning of crowdfunding for beginners.

The crowd in crowdfunding refers to ordinary, everyday people like you and me. The entire premise of crowdfunding evolves around common people. But why is it so successful, you might ask? See, raising money from people is not really about your business goals or your market knowledge, or even your product's forecasts: it's about trust and the ability to deliver what you say you can. People don't mind donating a few bucks to charity or lending their friends another couple of bucks.

However, it's not quite the same situation when the amount involved ranges in thousands of bucks.

This is where crowdfunding really comes into play. It can help small businesses or start-ups to raise money for their next big project, which could greatly improve people's lives and past-times. It does so by connecting a large crowd of people where they are free to invest in innovative products and services that they're interested in.

Crowdfunding also eliminates the technical and administrative hassles for those running crowdfunding campaigns, as the major platforms manage everything and provide lots of support to its users.

If you are looking for an effective solution to kick-start your passion project, nothing comes close to the competence of crowdfunding. The only catch is that you should have a great campaign that engages potential backers and entices them into backing your campaign. If you're hesitant about how that would work out for you, you can consult an advertising agency in London. They are professionals with all the talents, experience and means required to give your campaign a very valuable head start.

Plus, nowadays there are so many options for crowdfunding. That makes it all the better because you can choose something that works best for you and your product. For example, Kickstarter is one of the pioneers and by far the most popular crowdfunding platform. The advantage of kickstarter is that it has SO many users. You will really have "crowds" at your disposal. The problem is that so many people want to raise money there that it can be difficult for your project to become visible. Thus, kickstarter is great if you already have some type of fan base that can get you going and raise the profile and popularity of your project. Once you get the ball rolling, it can really take off and go viral.

Indiegogo is another option for more outside of the box projects. One of the advantages here is that Indiegogo allows you to keep whatever you've raised even if you don't hit your goal. Kickstarter does not. If you don't hit your goal, you don't get anything.

Traditionally, the way crowdfunding works is that people invest early in your product before it's been made or developed. They are providing the funds you need to launch your business and get the product developed.

So what's in it for them? Apart from the sense of community and excitement of being part of something cutting edge, people are actually buying the product. And they're getting it for a great discount. For example if your project is a special new kind of binoculars and you need to raise $10,000 to launch your business and get the products manufactured, you can advertise on kickstarter that if people invest $10 in the binoculars, they'll receive a pair. When you actually launch the business, you'll be selling the binoculars for $20 so people are getting a great deal if they invest early and help you fund the project.

Another option that some crowdfunding platforms offer makes it much more like venture capitalism. People can fund your project or business in exchange for equity in the business. This means they will become part owner. This is probably the biggest motivation of all if someone believes in your business they may be willing to fork over large sums and get your project off the ground if they can own a piece of it.

As you can see, the options are limitless and you have many options here. Crowdfunding really is a form of social media marketing and can create huge hype for your business. It's definitely worth considering depending on your product/business type.

Conclusion

Technology is changing our lives in so many ways. Ways that only a generation ago were figments of the imagination. Of course, the single biggest change is the Internet, which has pretty much leveled the playing field – in terms of marketing - and has also made business more competitive than ever.

As you learned in this book, social media marketing is an indirect way of selling – compared to traditional marketing – and primarily engages prospects and customers using high quality and unique content, which makes them feel increasingly more connected to products and services. Particularly with Facebook, social media marketing can help you reach more of your intended market at significantly lower cost than traditional marketing. Talk about the most bang for your marketing bucks!

To be done successfully, we learned that social media marketing must target your customers as individuals and make them feel valued and engaged. It involves more creative and entertaining ideas than traditional marketing to really get people excited about your brand and make them become not just a customer, but a "fan," or an "advocate," or an "ambassador" of your brand. It also involves a more personal touch and therefore greater degrees of friendliness and sociability. Gaining the loyalty and trust of your customers is the ultimate goal and great social media marketing strategies can get you there.

Frankly, in this day in age, you simply can't afford not

to have a robust social media marketing presence because this is the wave of the future. In fact, the future is already here!

Not to say there's no value left in traditional marketing but social media marketing is just a completely different animal. It breaks all the rules and challenges all the norms.

One of the biggest reasons most new businesses fail is failure to reach their intended market. Many businesses funnel hundreds of thousands of dollars into traditional marketing methods to connect with an already saturated market.

If you're spending more time and money on paid advertising and traditional advertising, than you are on social media marketing, you're going to fail. It's that simple. Even if you think it's a temporary, spur of the moment sort of fad, you need to come to terms with the fact that social media is here to stay, and it's a powerful force to be reckoned with. The benefits and rewards have endless potential, and the time and money you have to invest is low. Times have changed, and this is a part of the reality we live in now. Part of running a successful business is adaptability, so always remember that—even in your social media marketing strategies. Never get too comfortable. Always be ready to adapt and meet your customers at the next level.

This book has armed you with the tools and "know how" you need to take action. There's no time like the present to start implementing these 8 Pillars and watch how they transform your business.

52777047R00090

Made in the USA
Lexington, KY
19 September 2019